# CTHULHU vs BEAR

## The coloring book

By Mireille Sillander


ISBN 978-1500476656
For more information visit mireillesillander.weebly.com

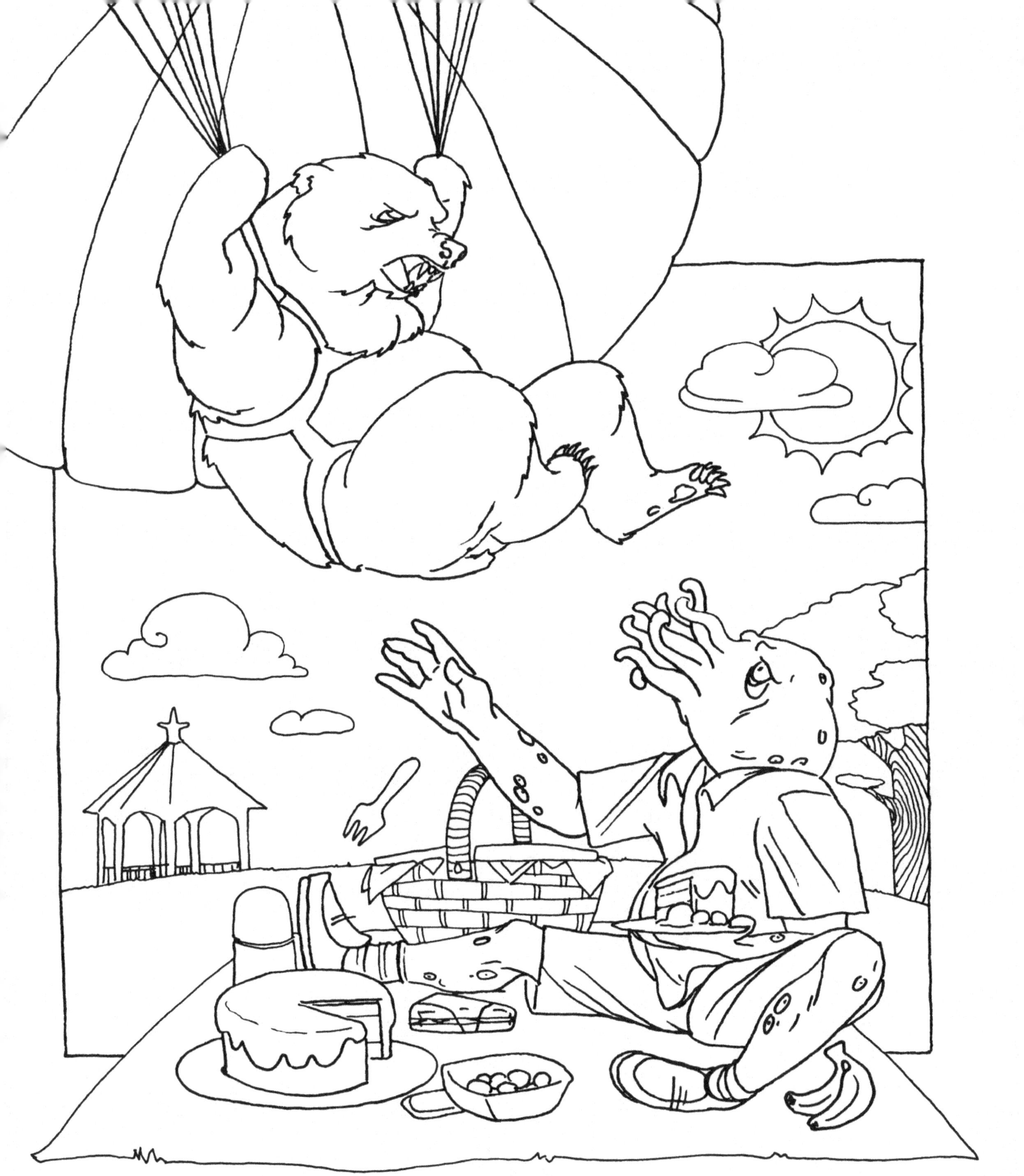

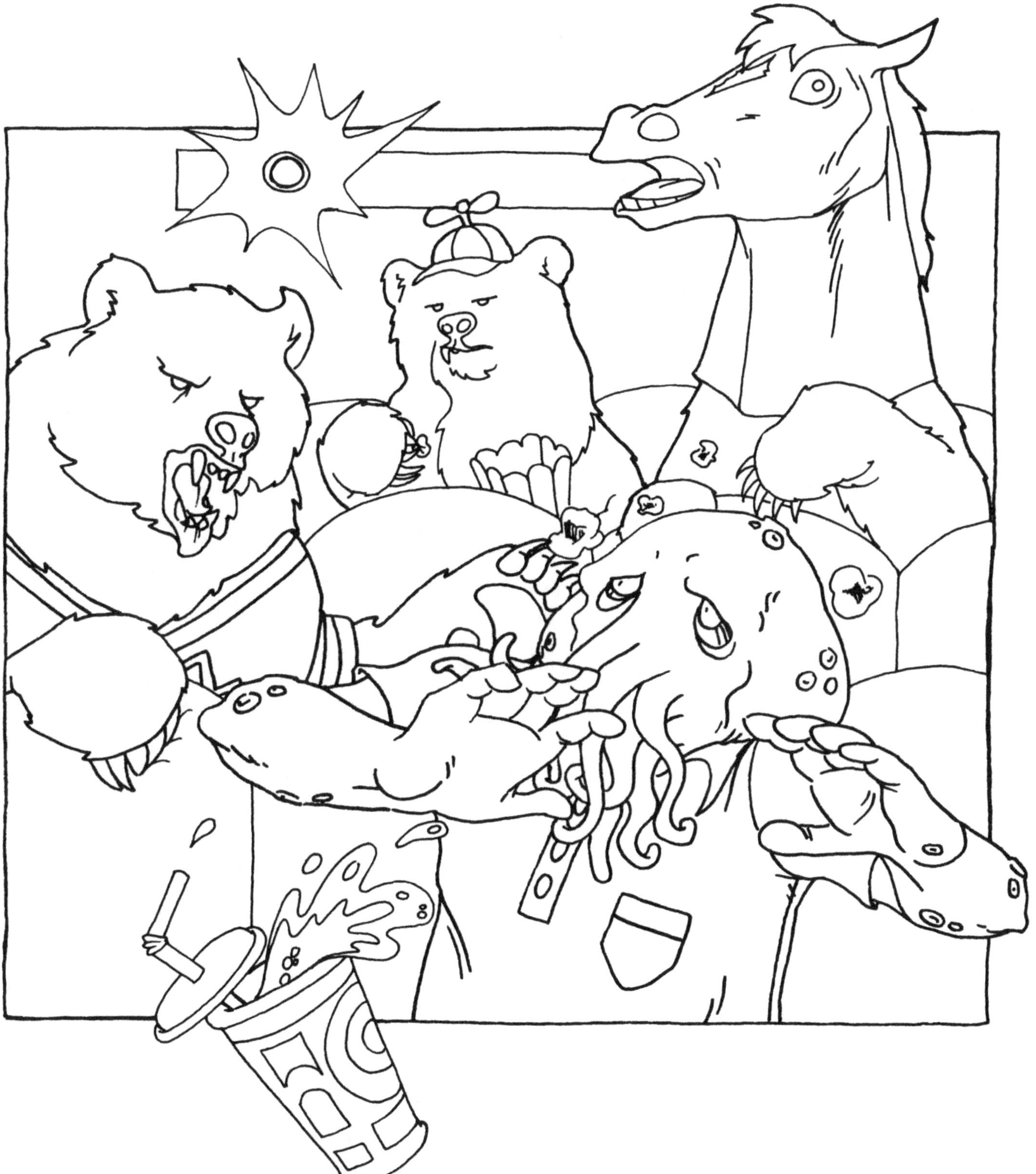

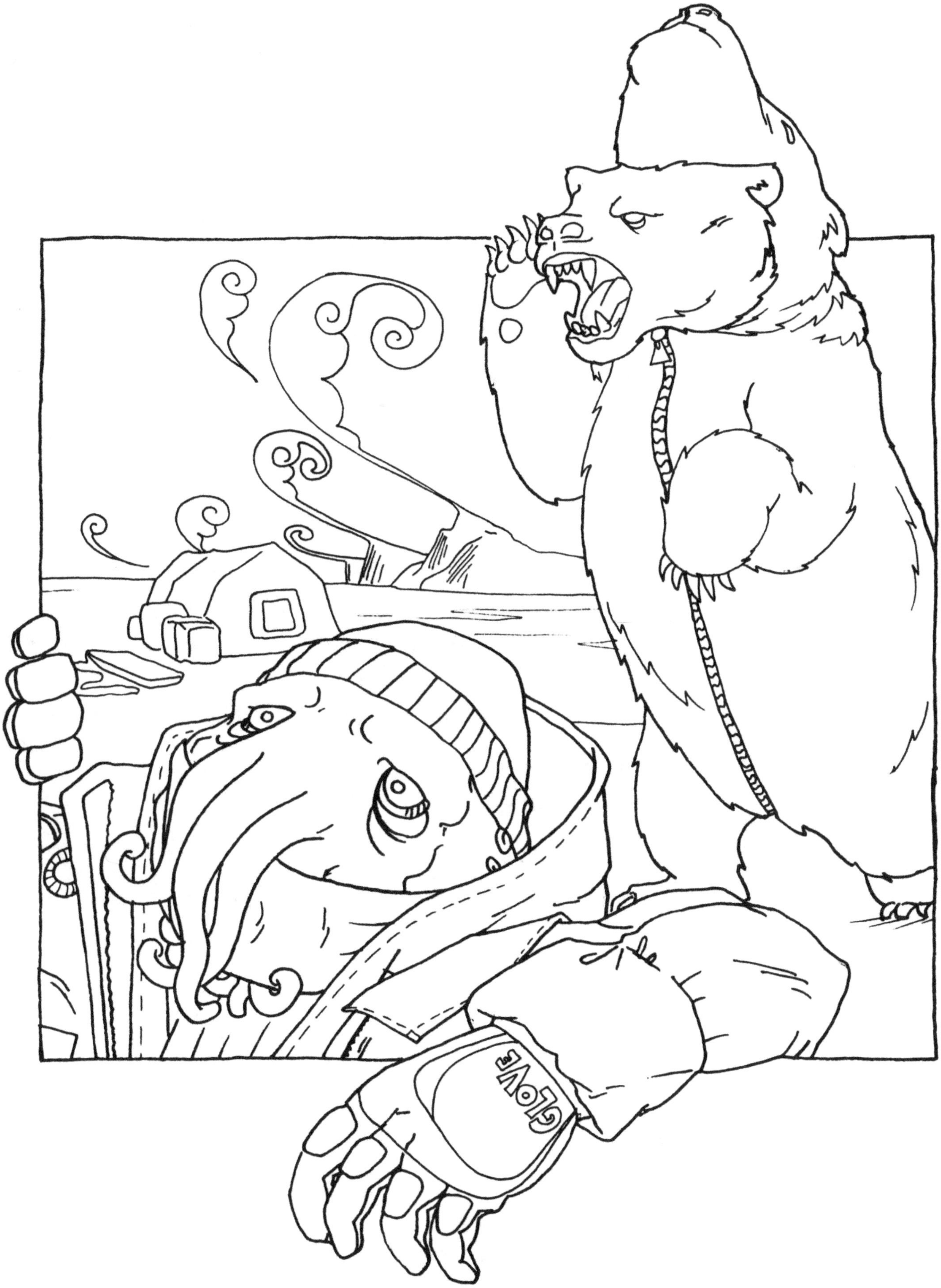

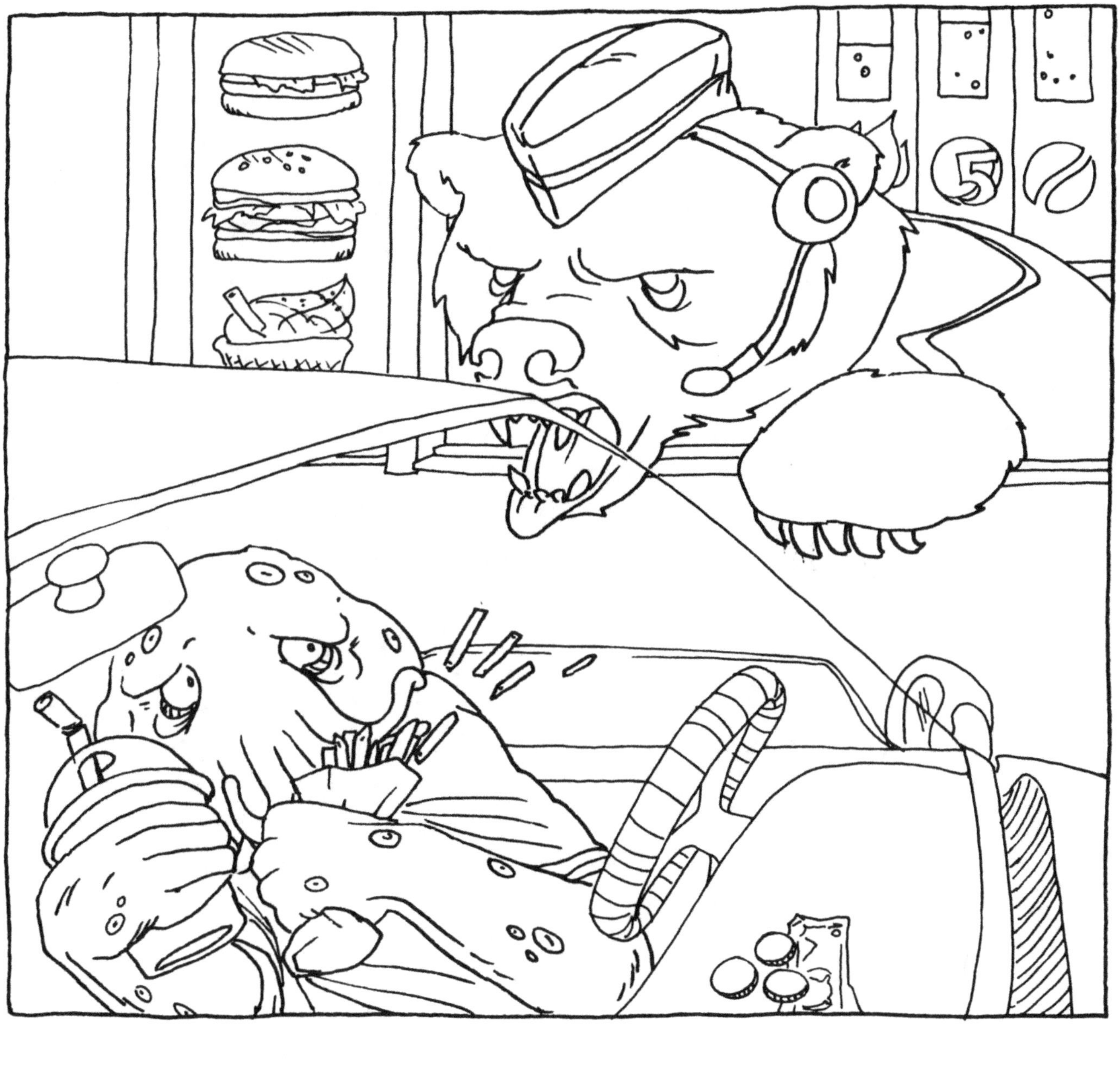
5

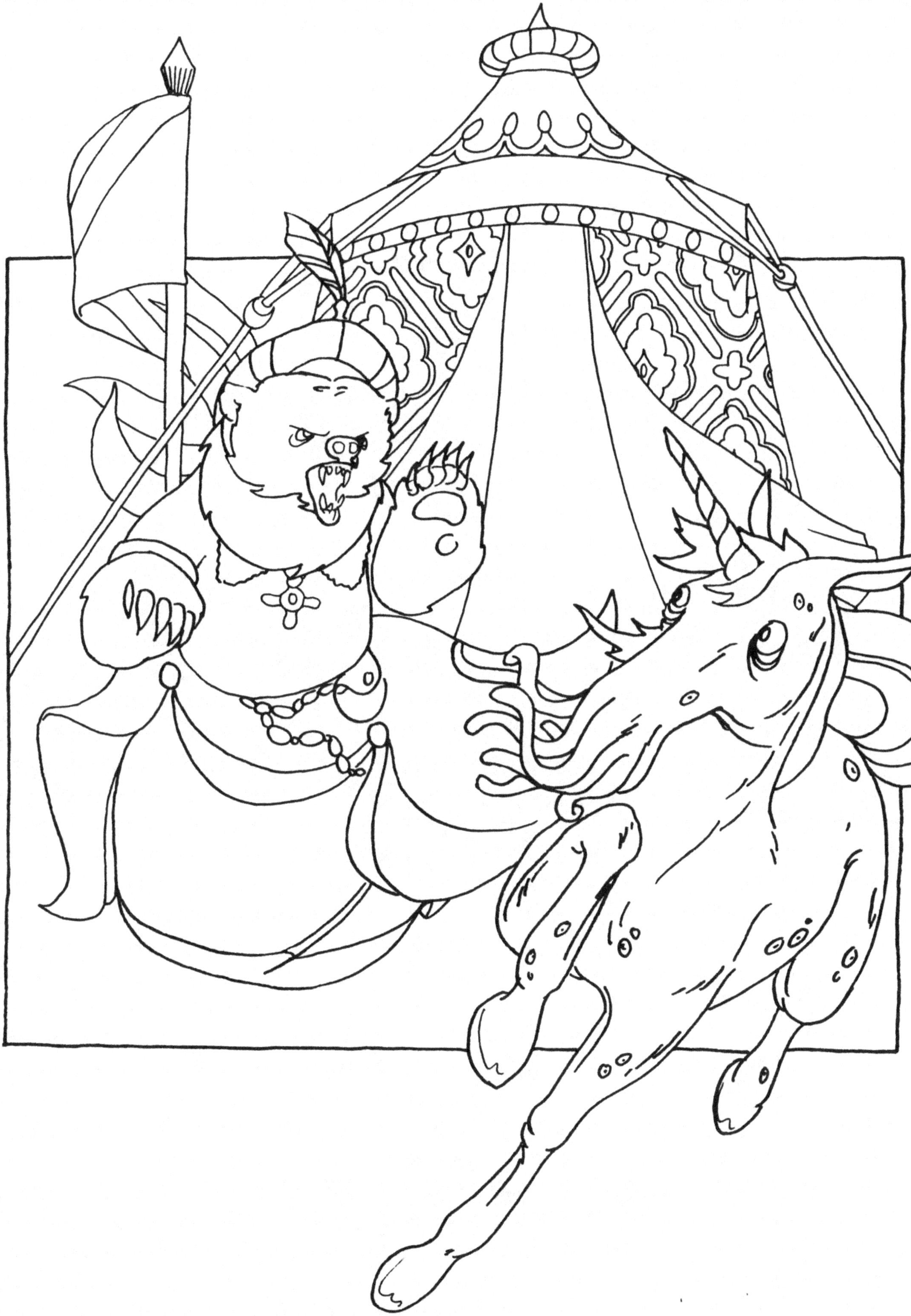

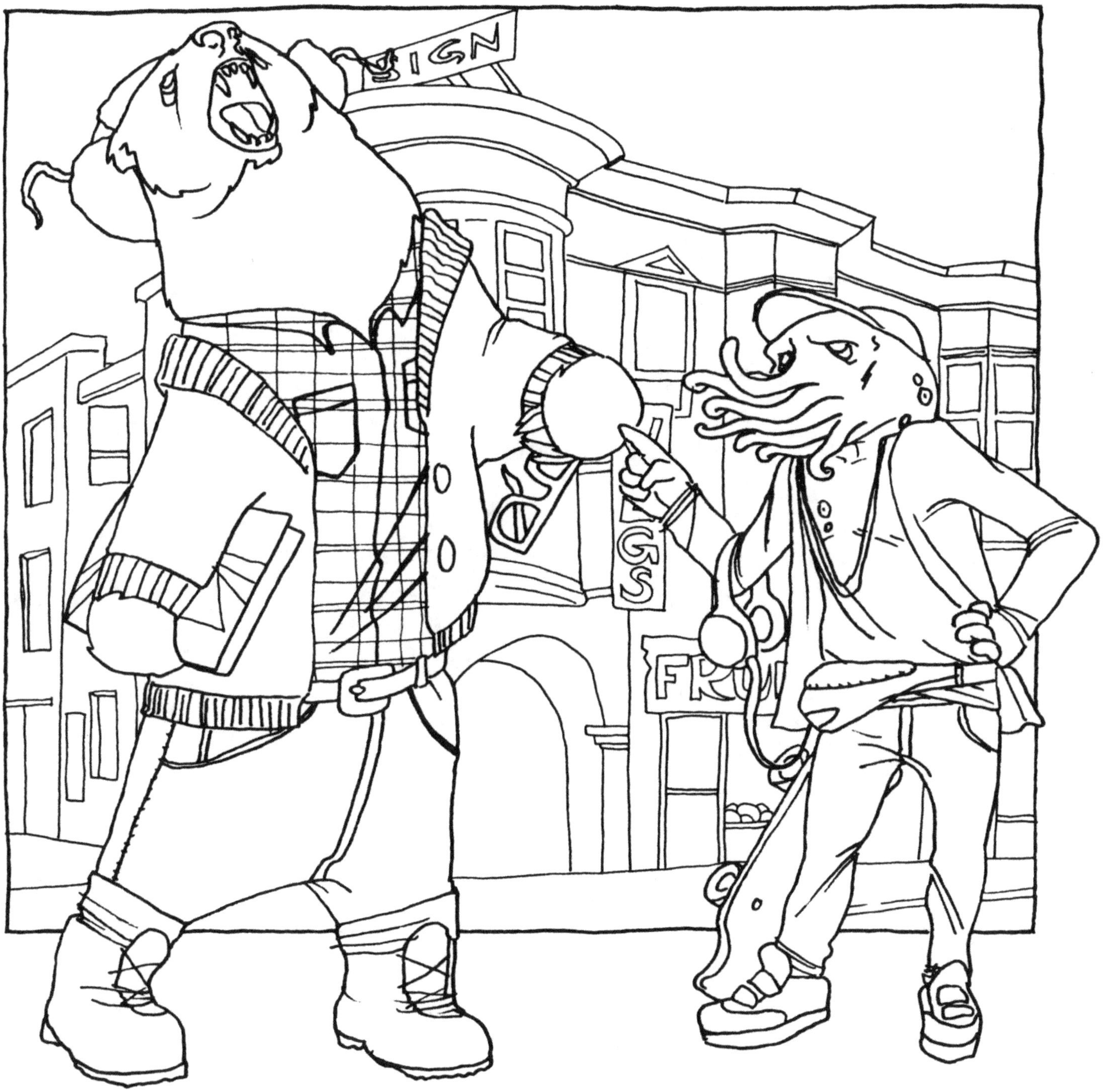
SIGN
GS
FRU

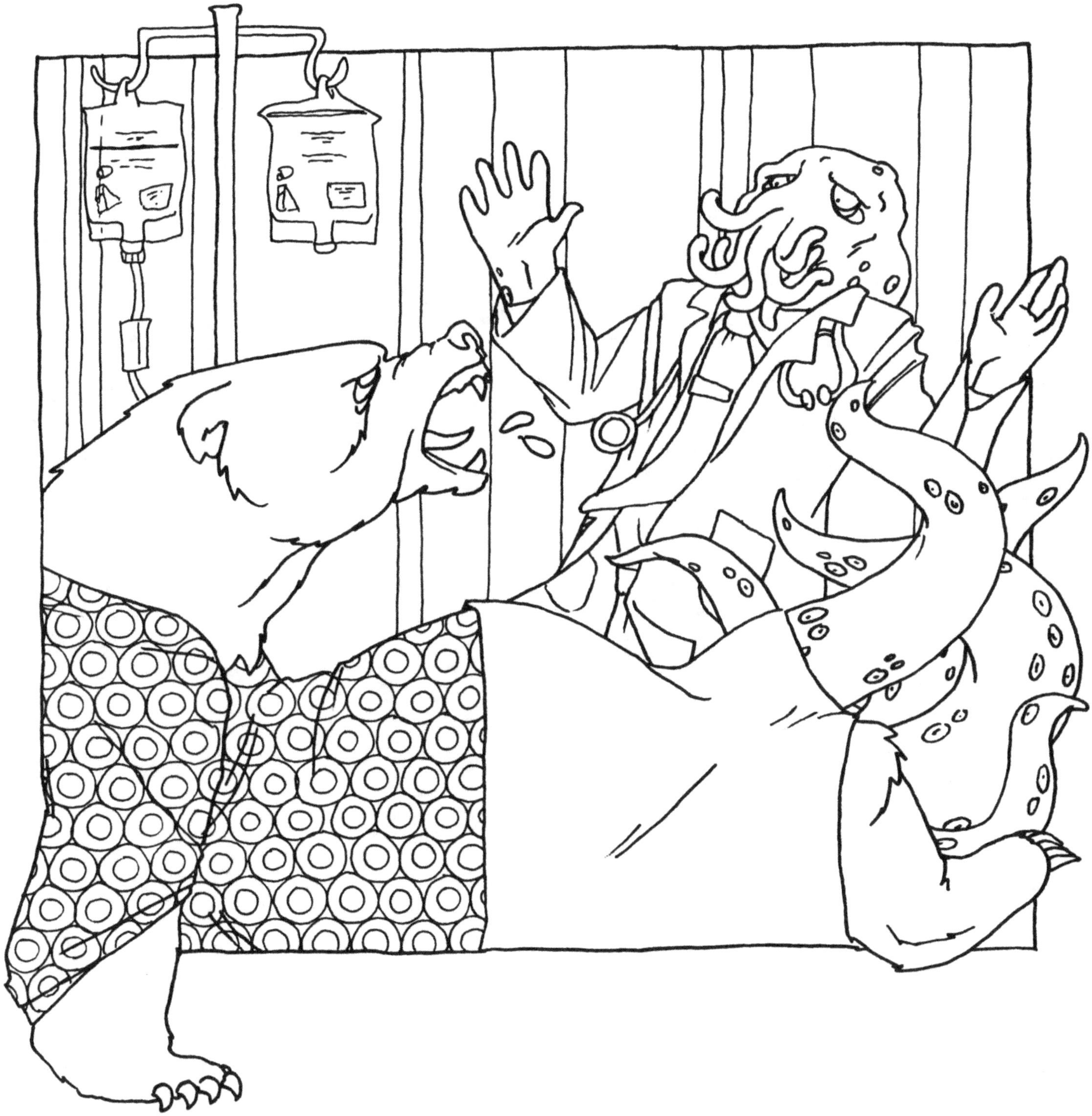

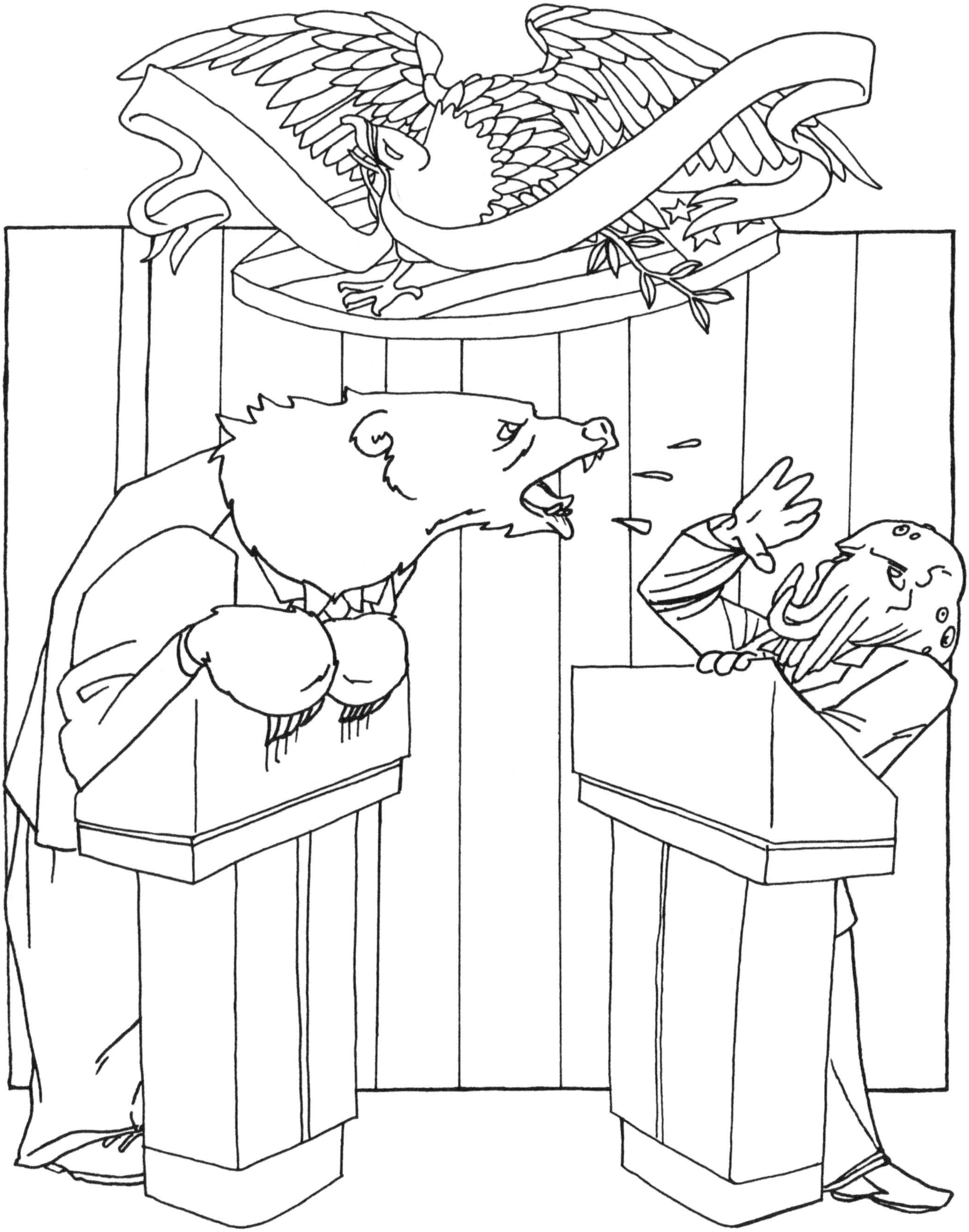

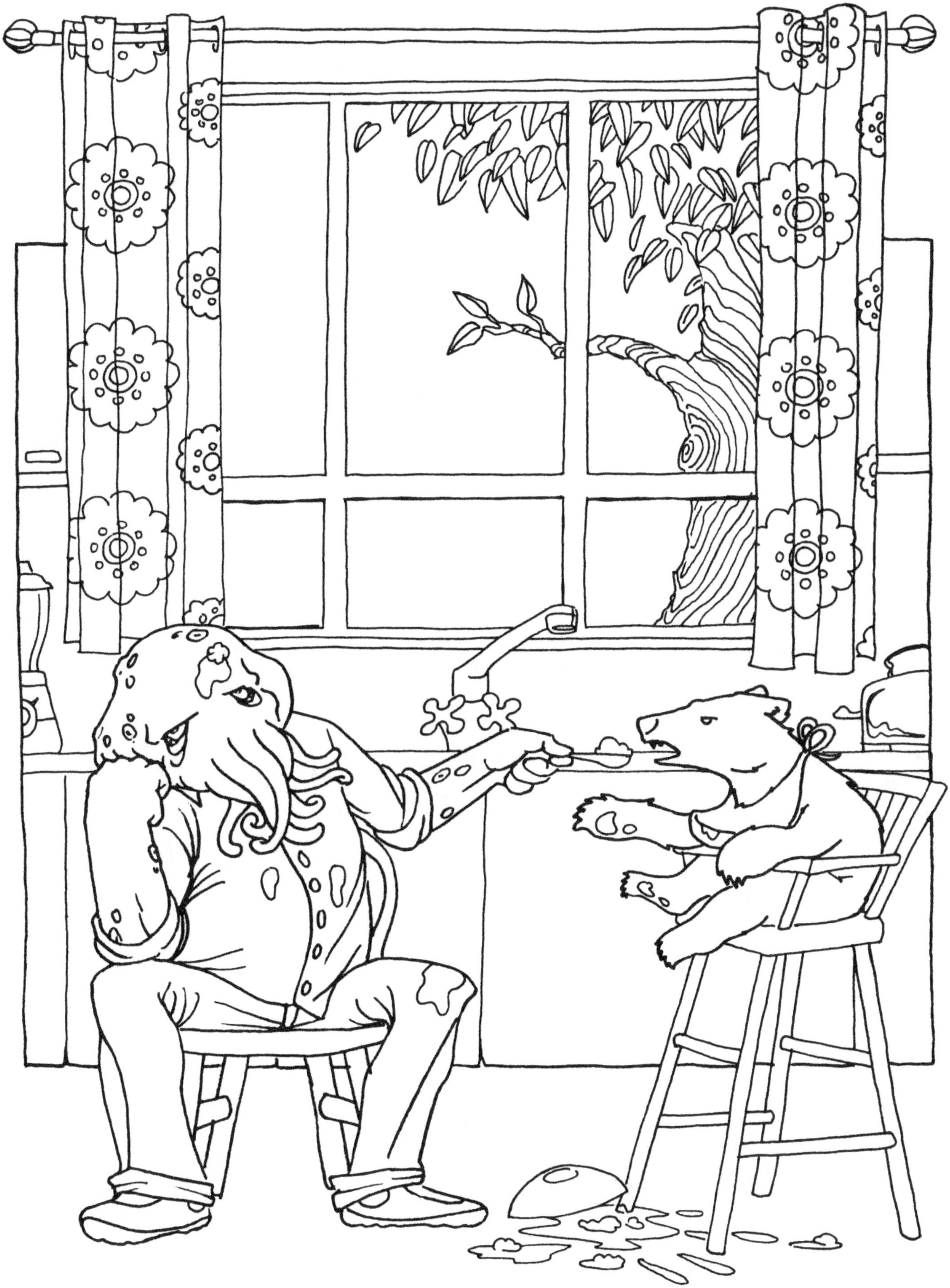

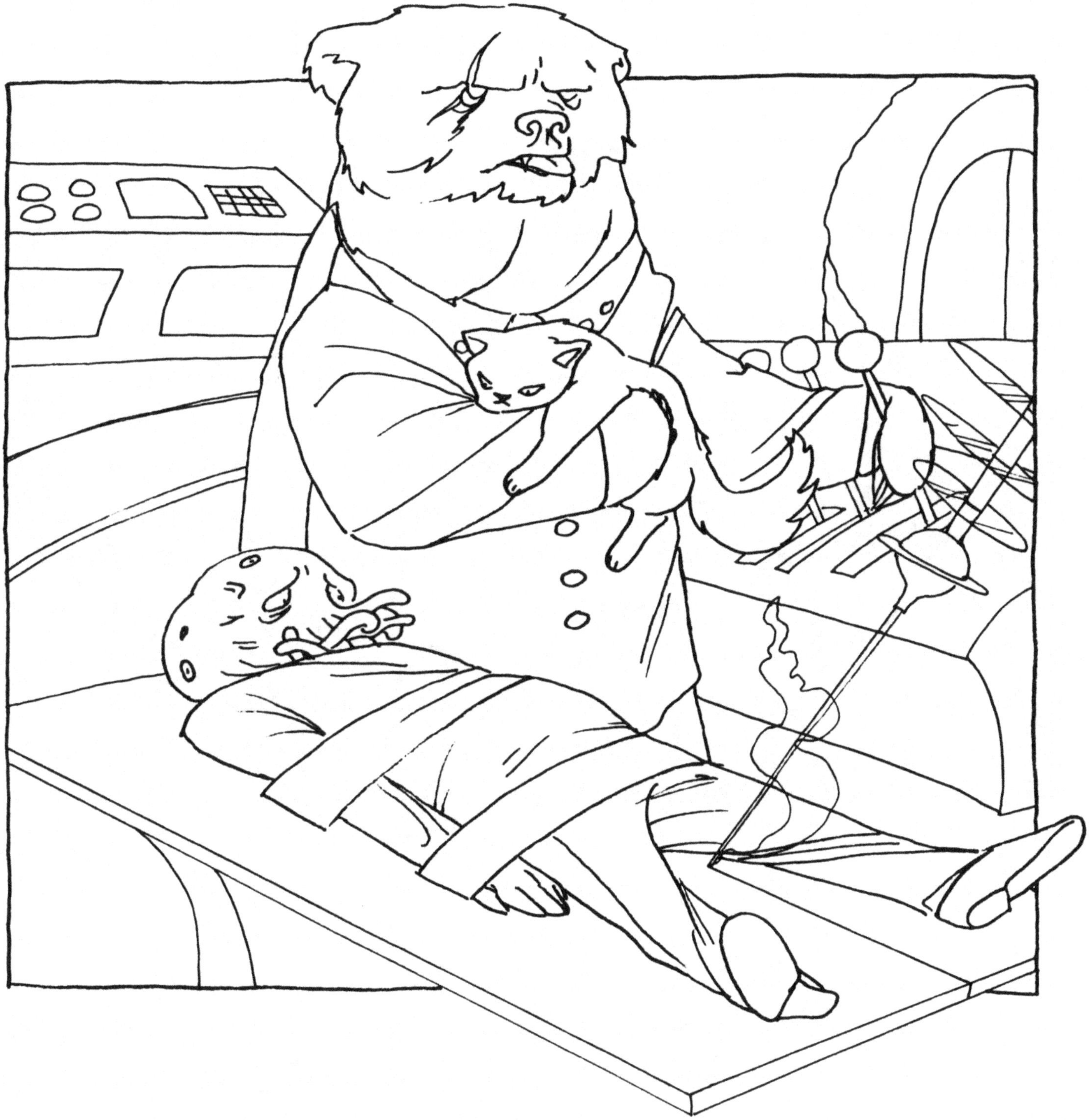

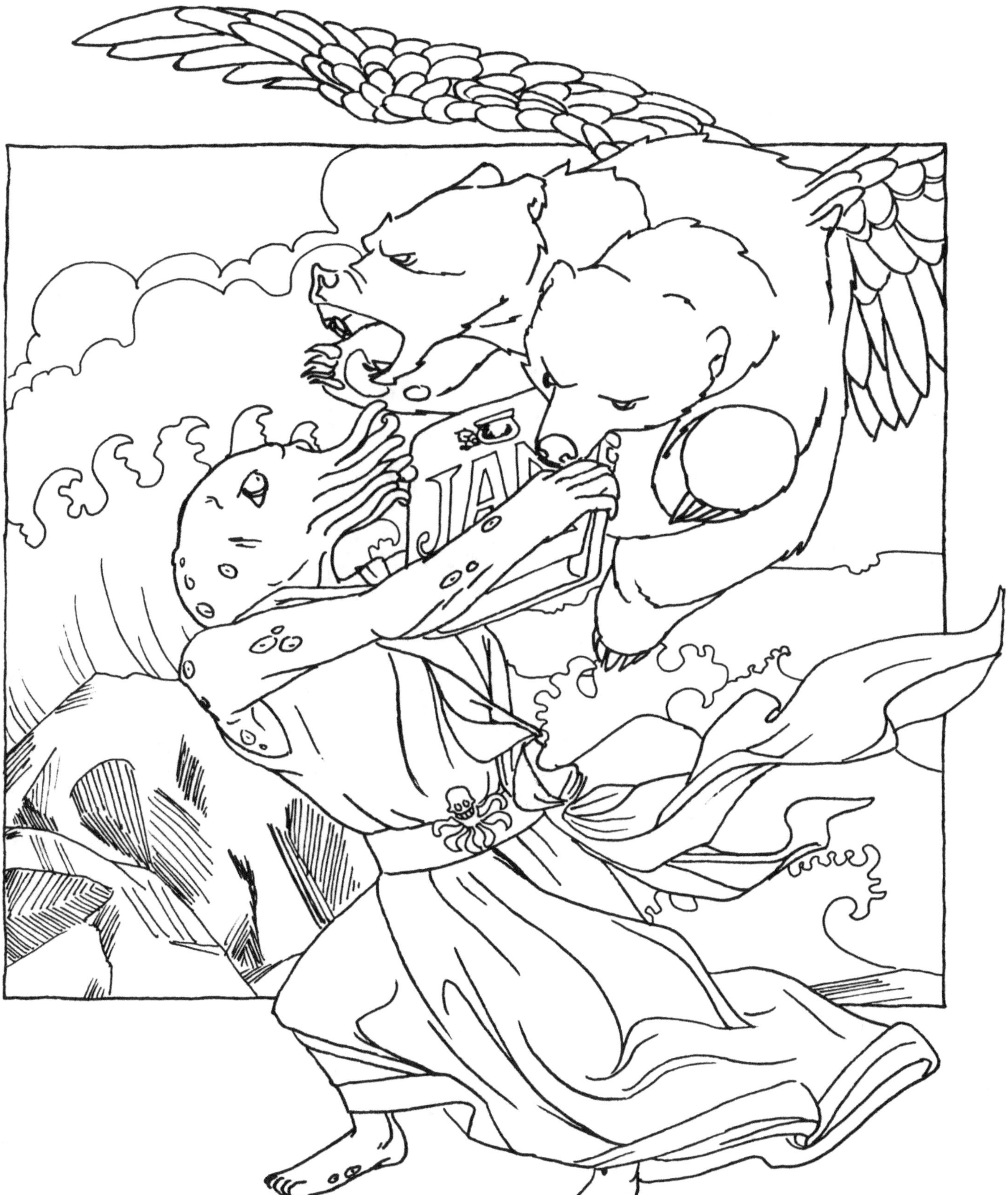

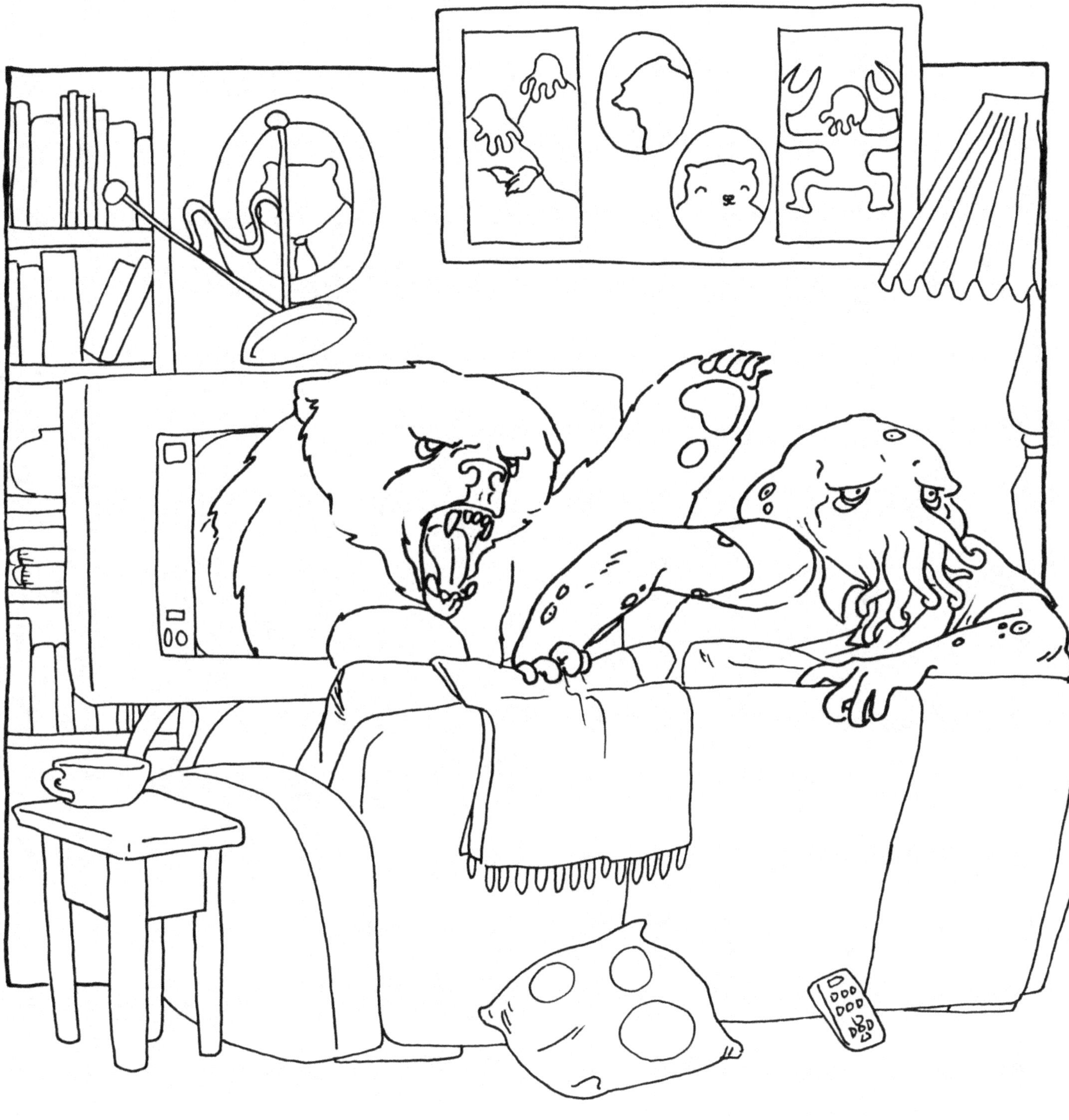

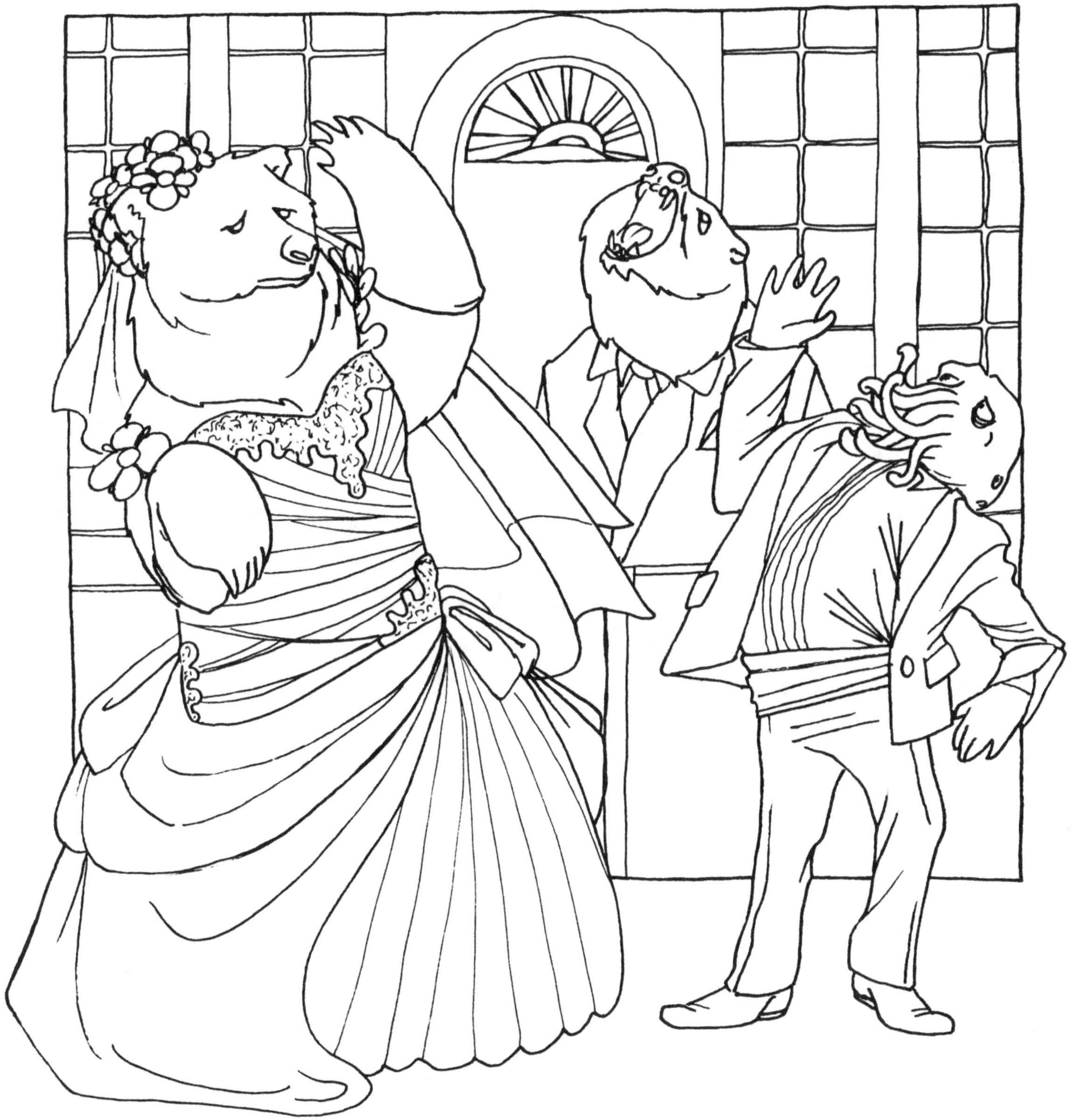

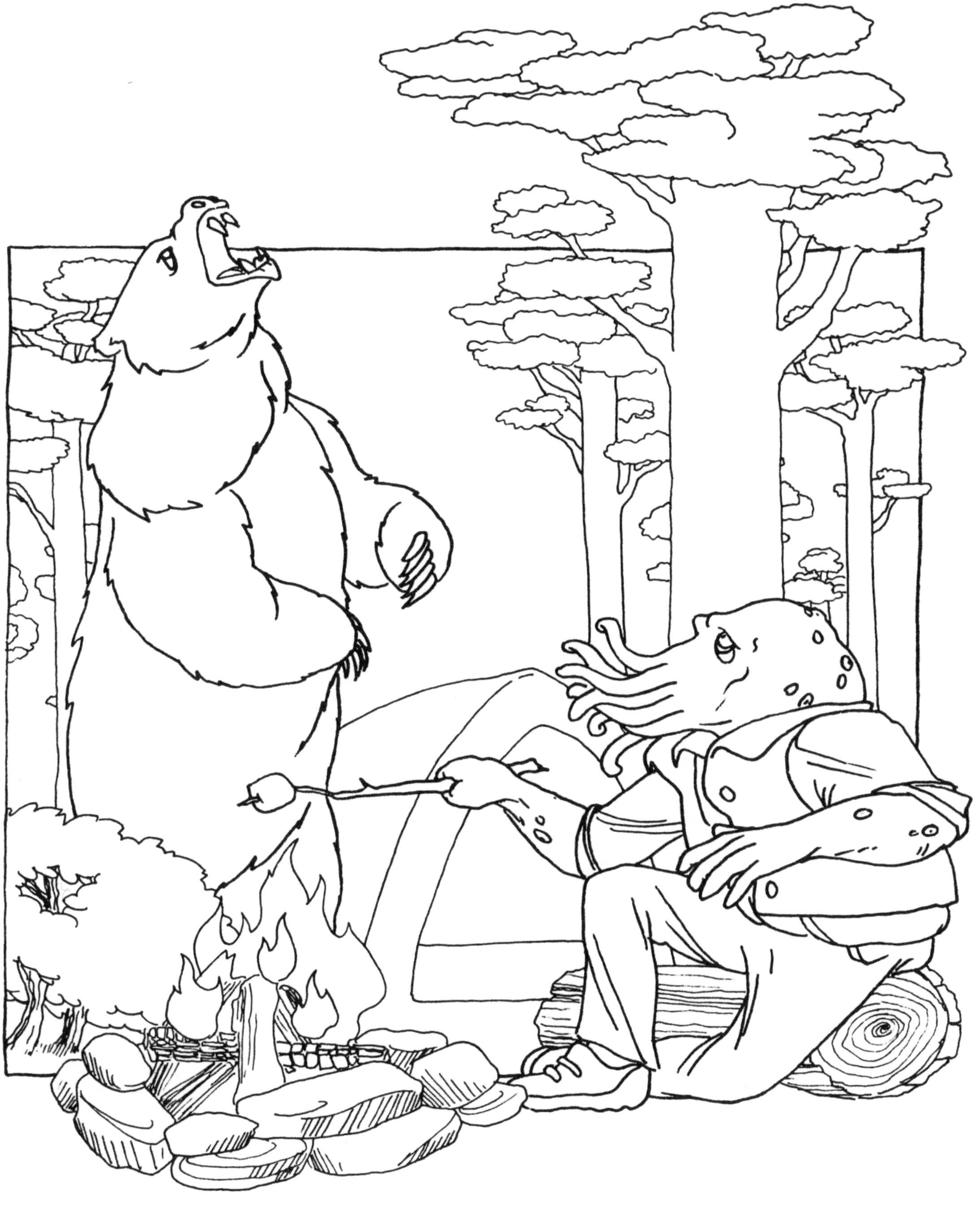

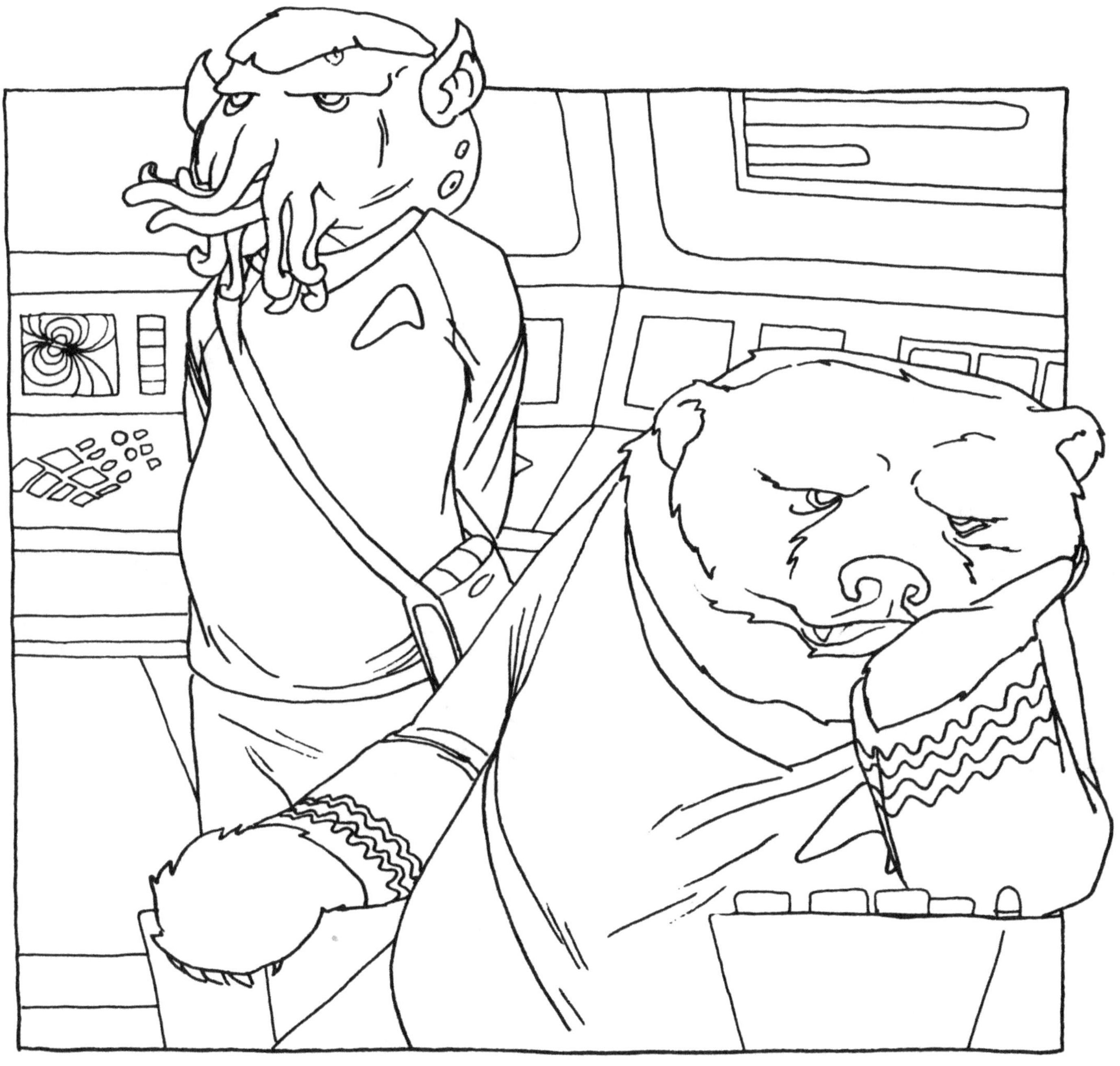

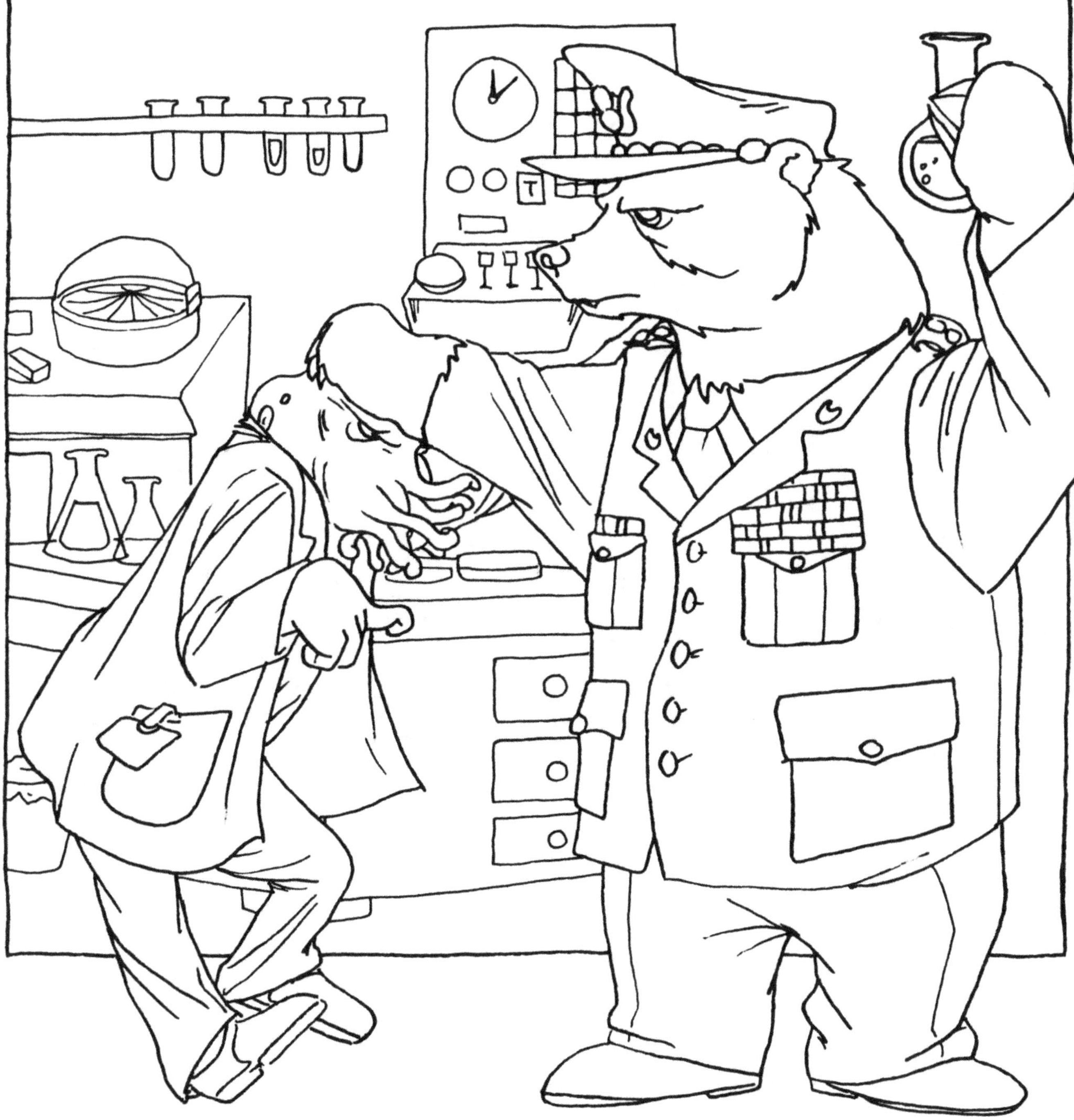

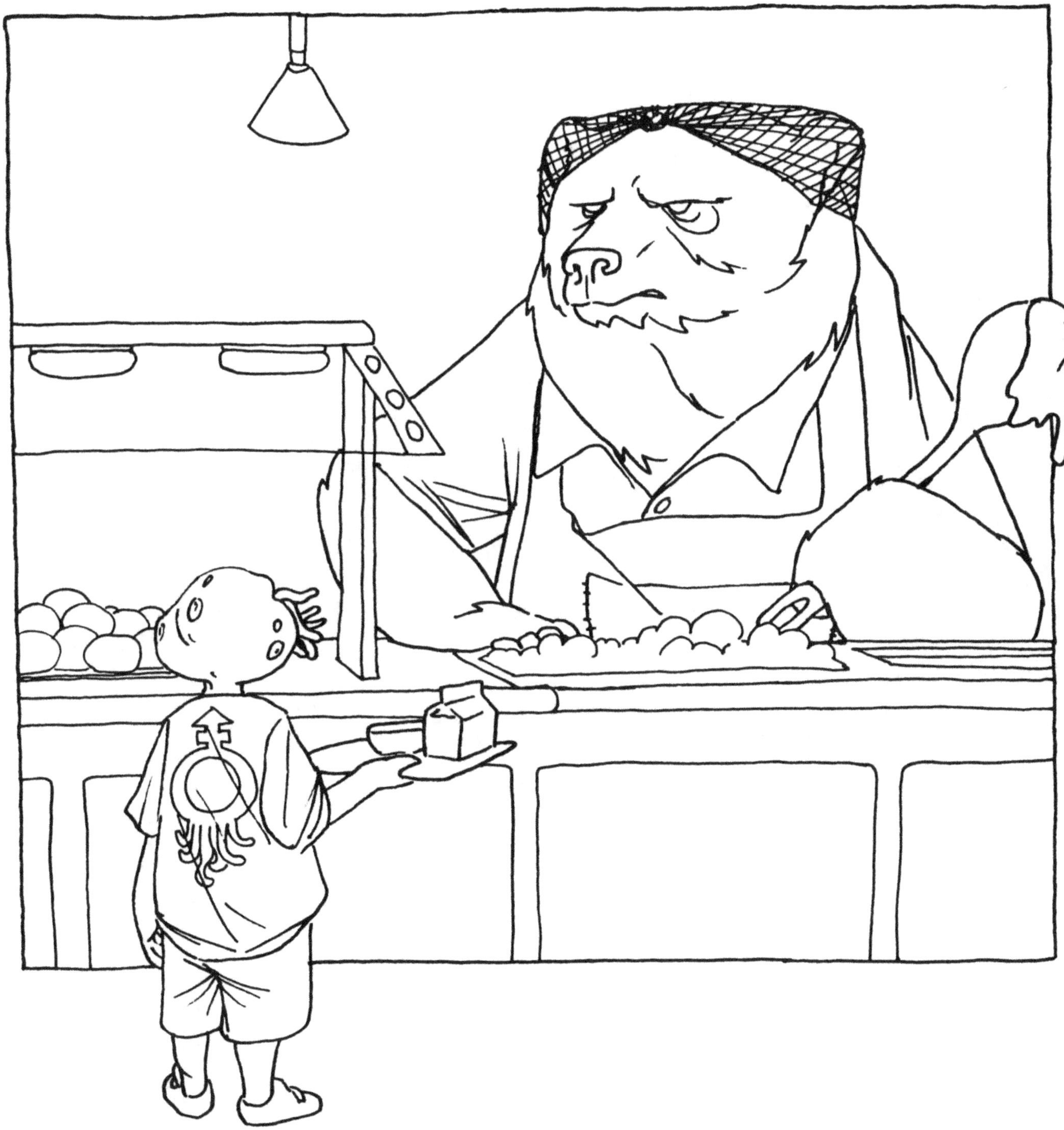

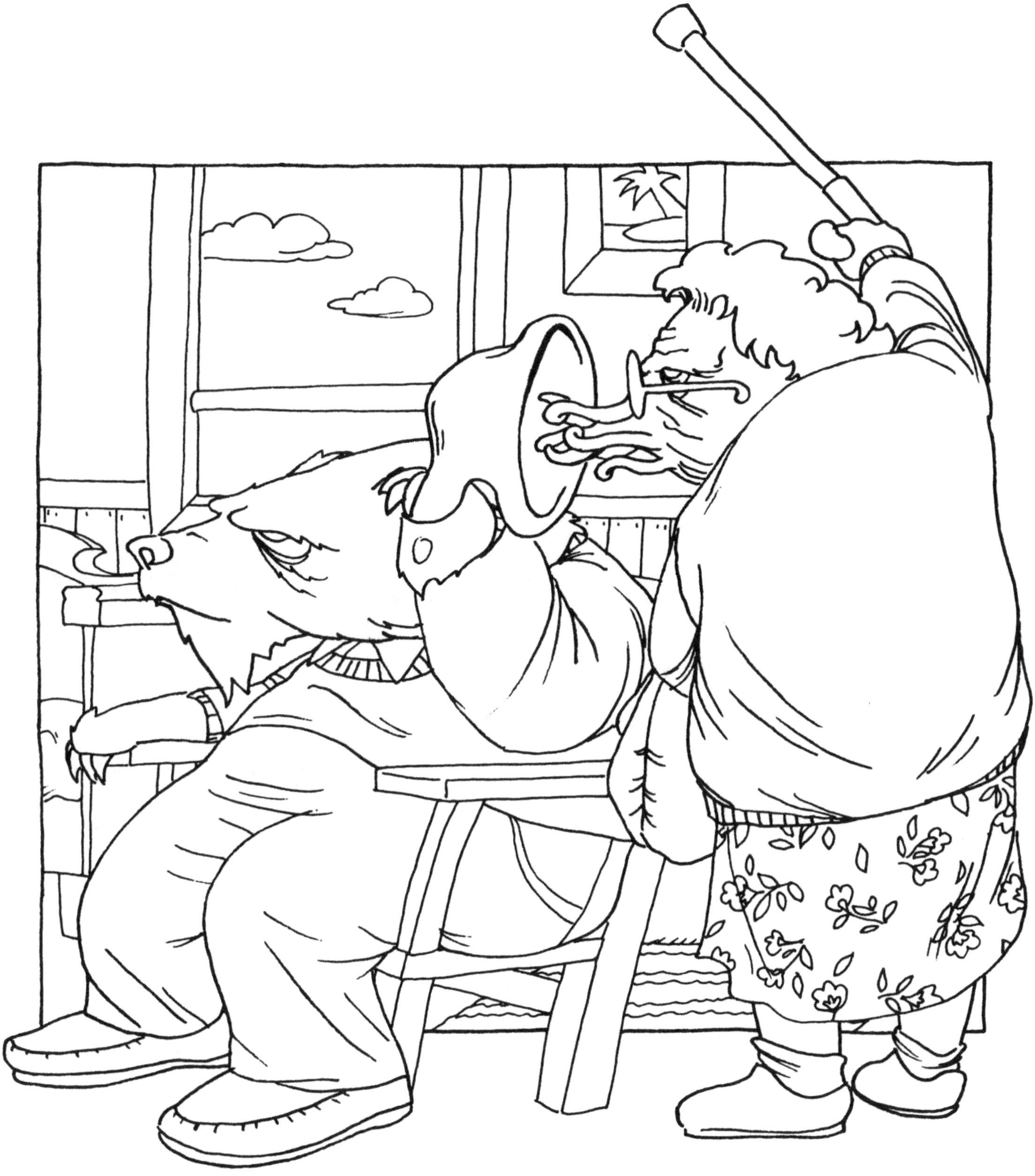

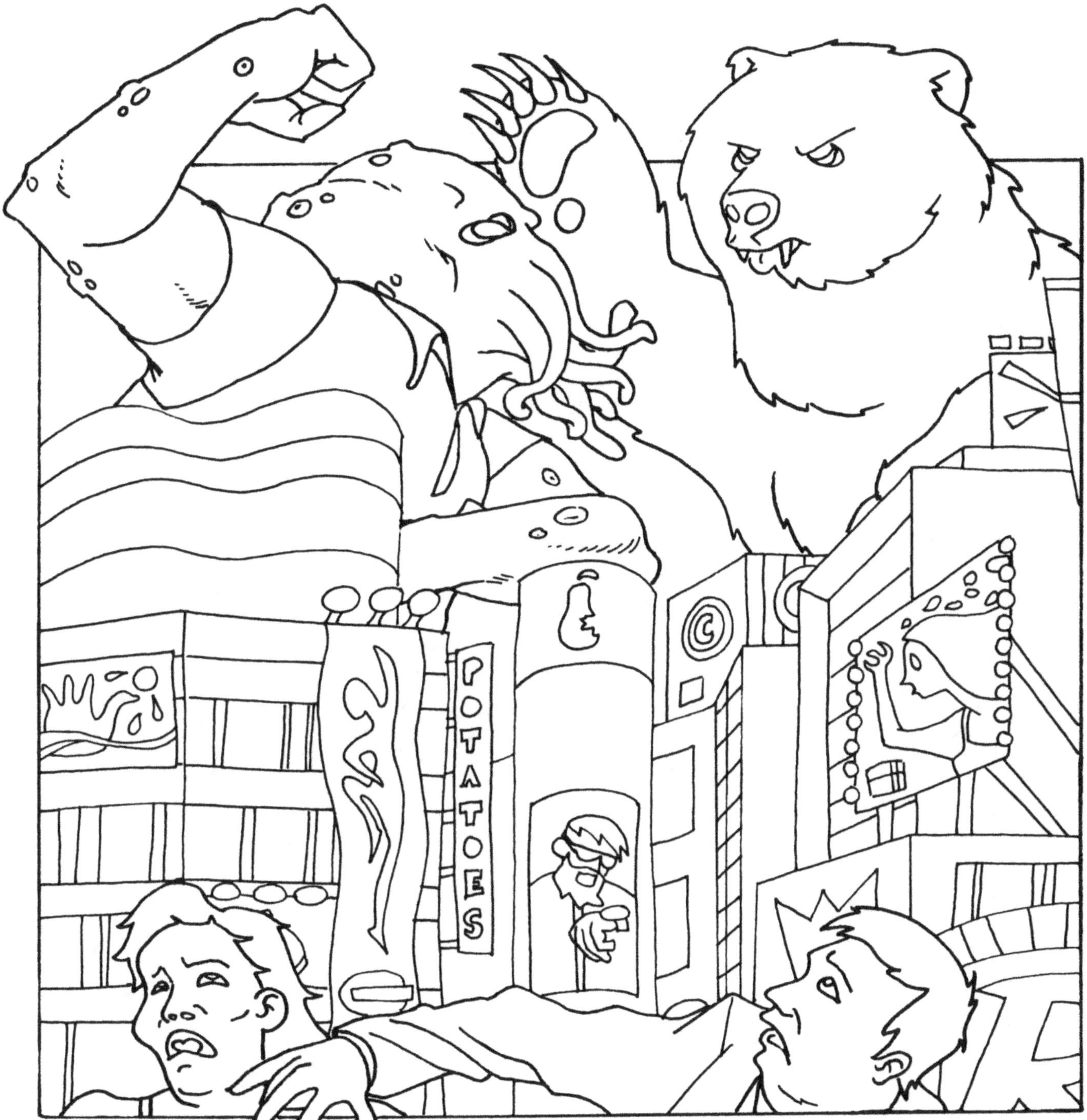
POTATOES

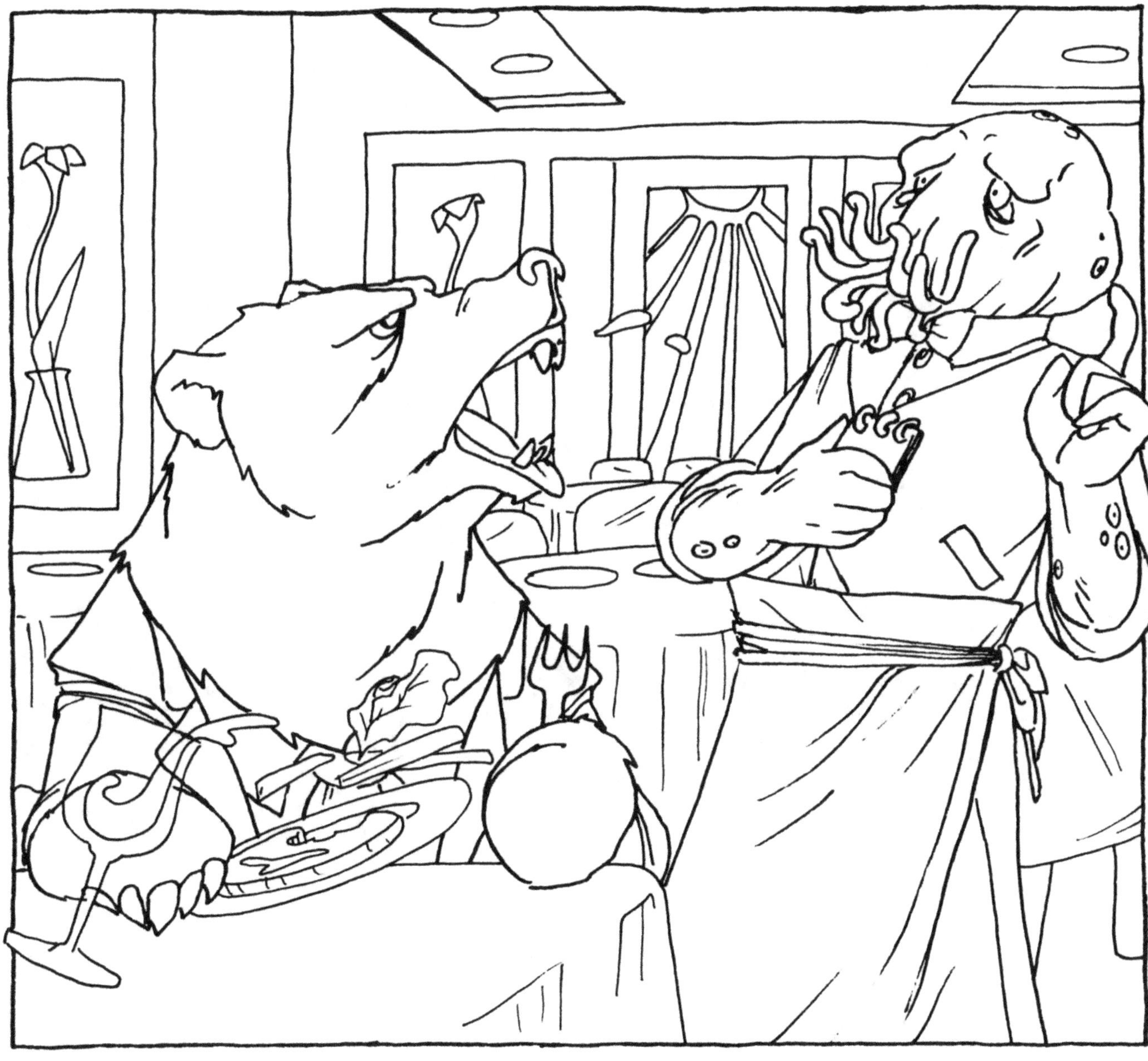

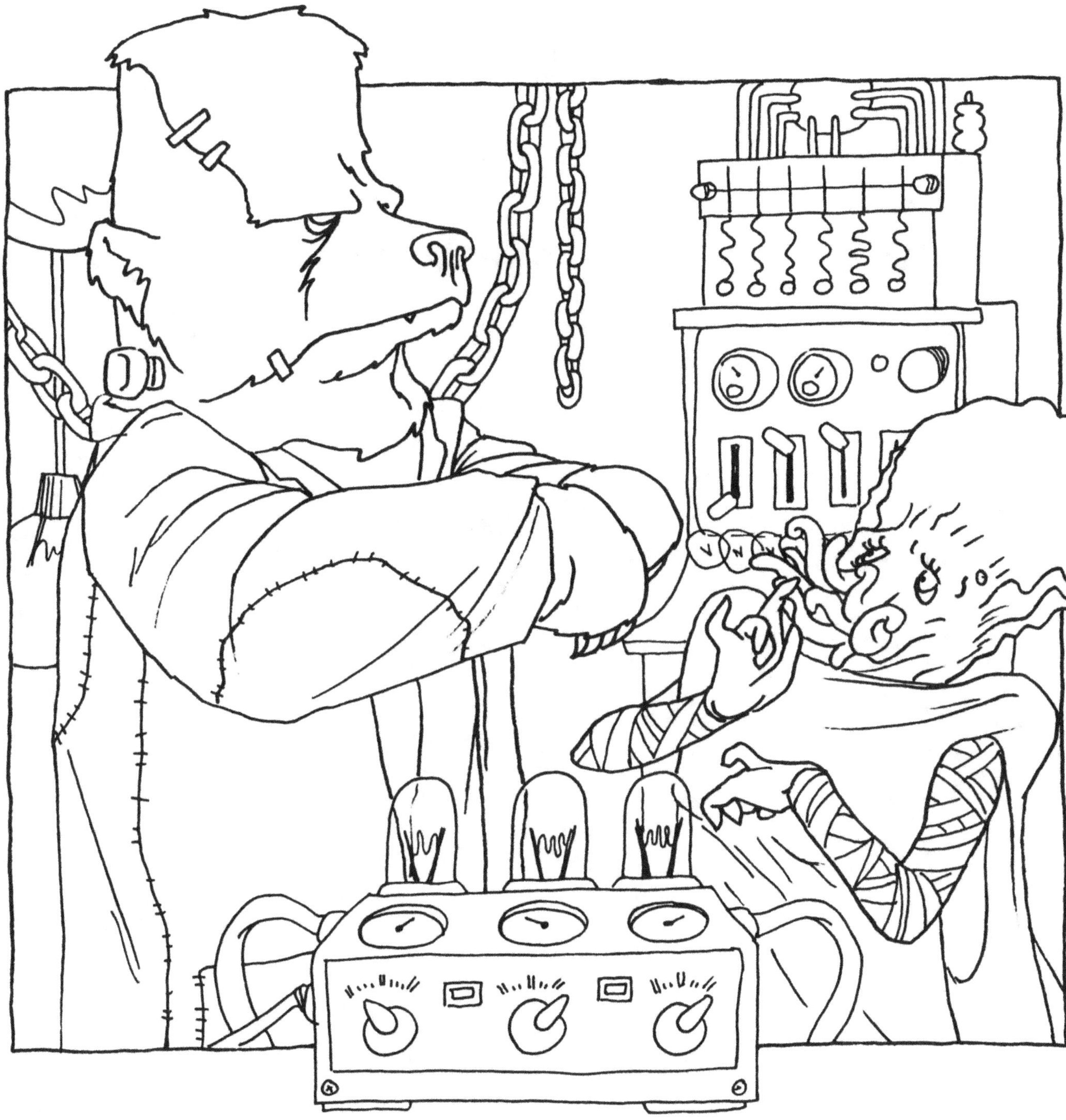

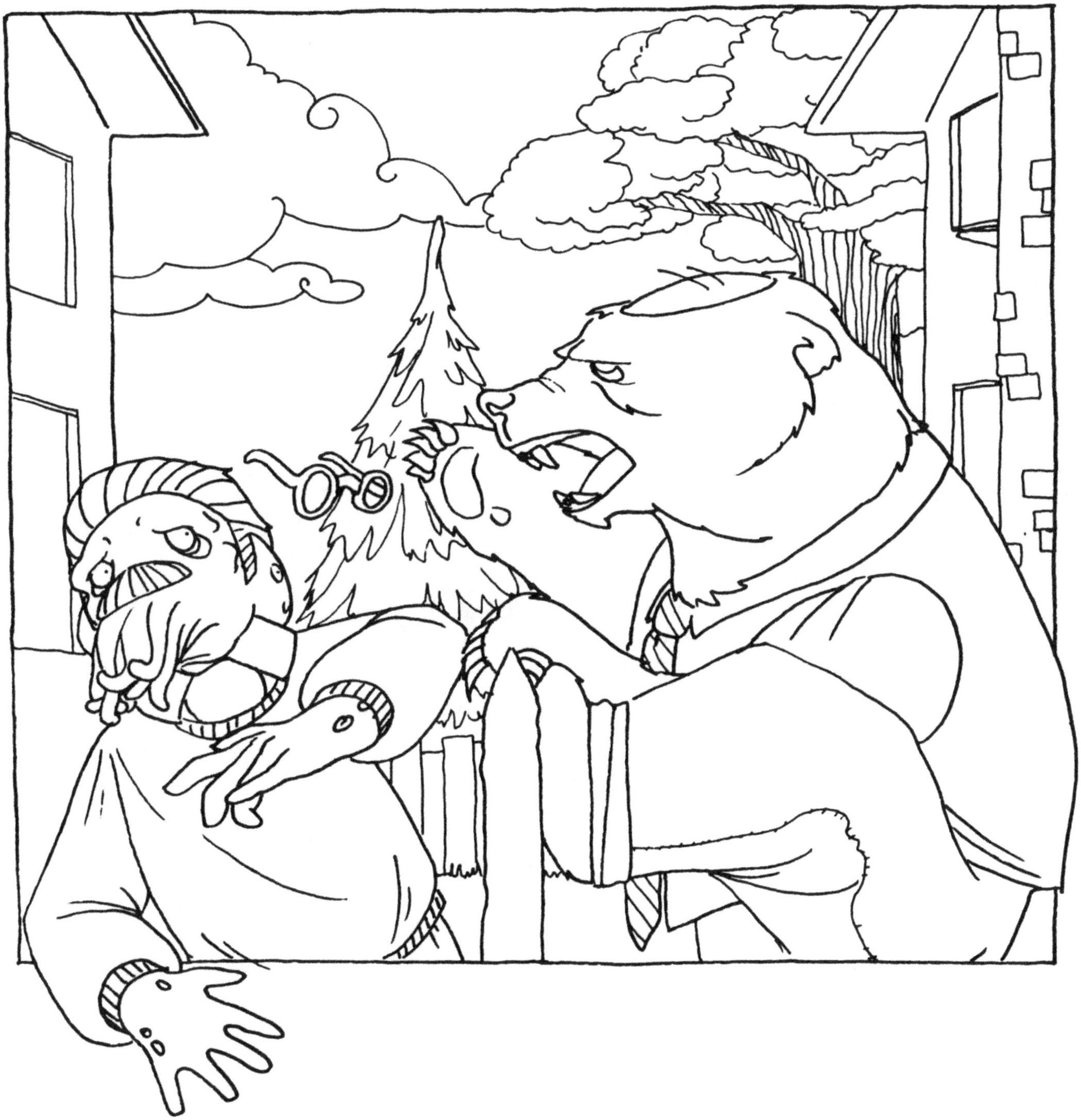

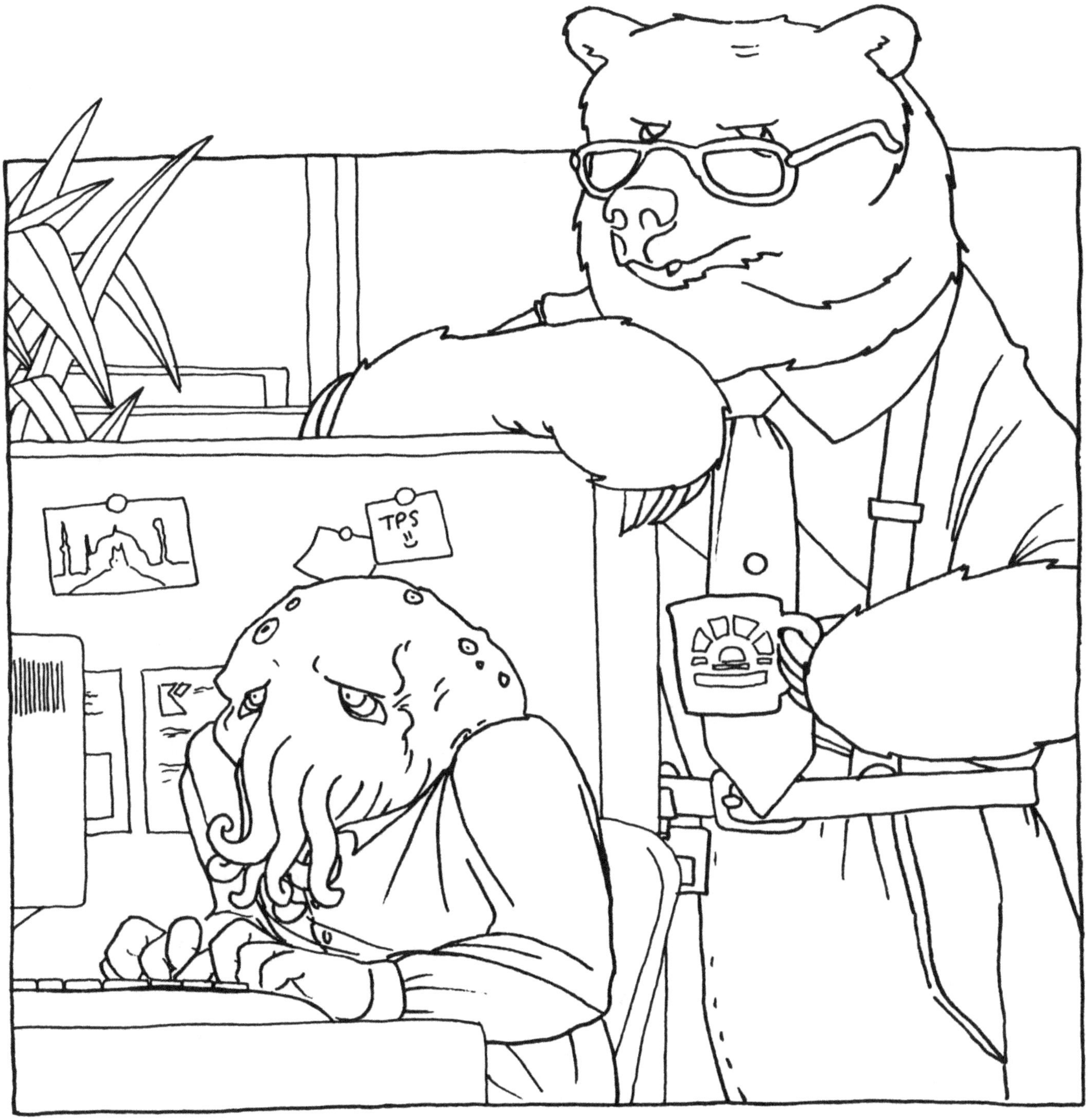
TPS

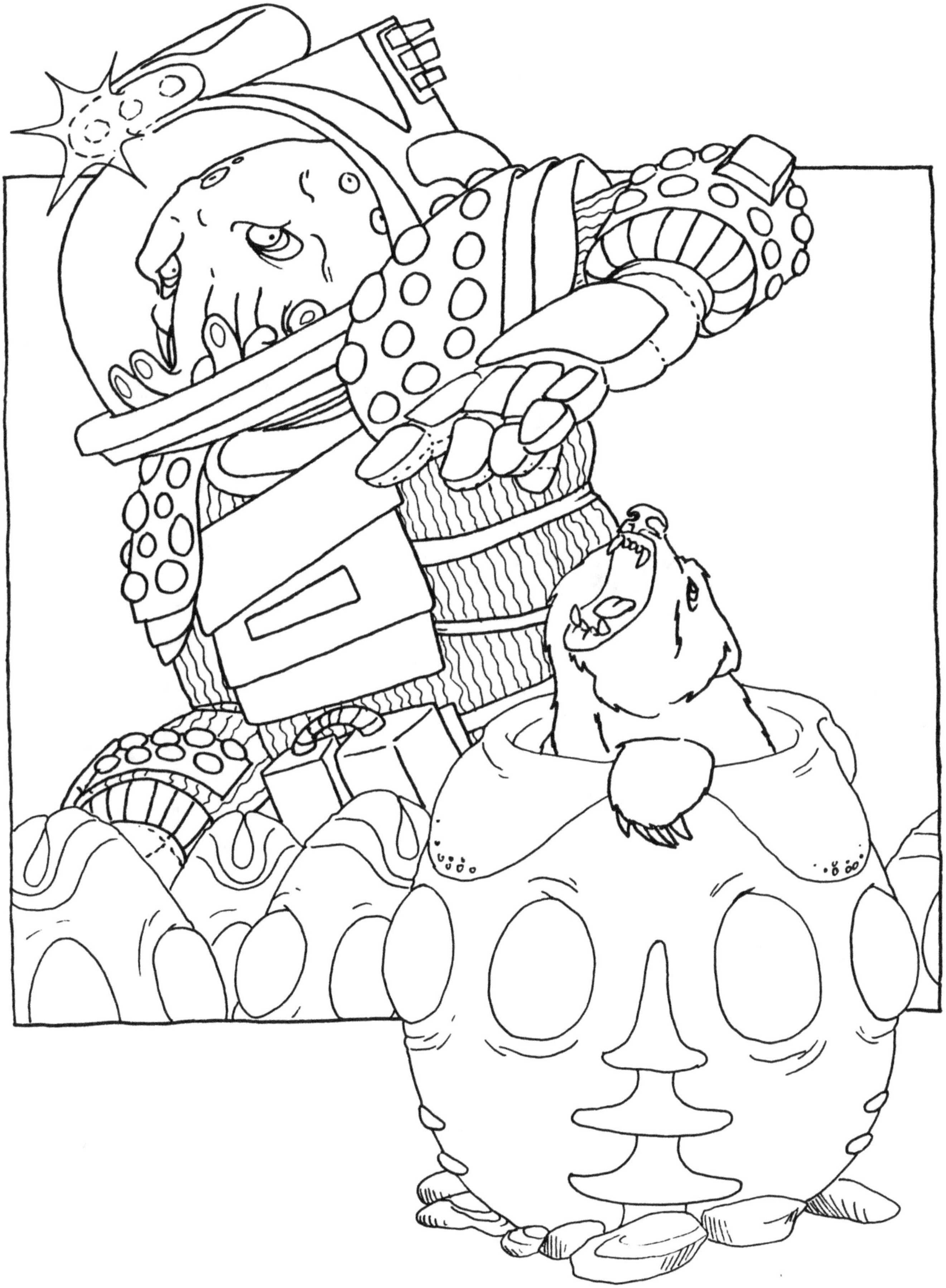

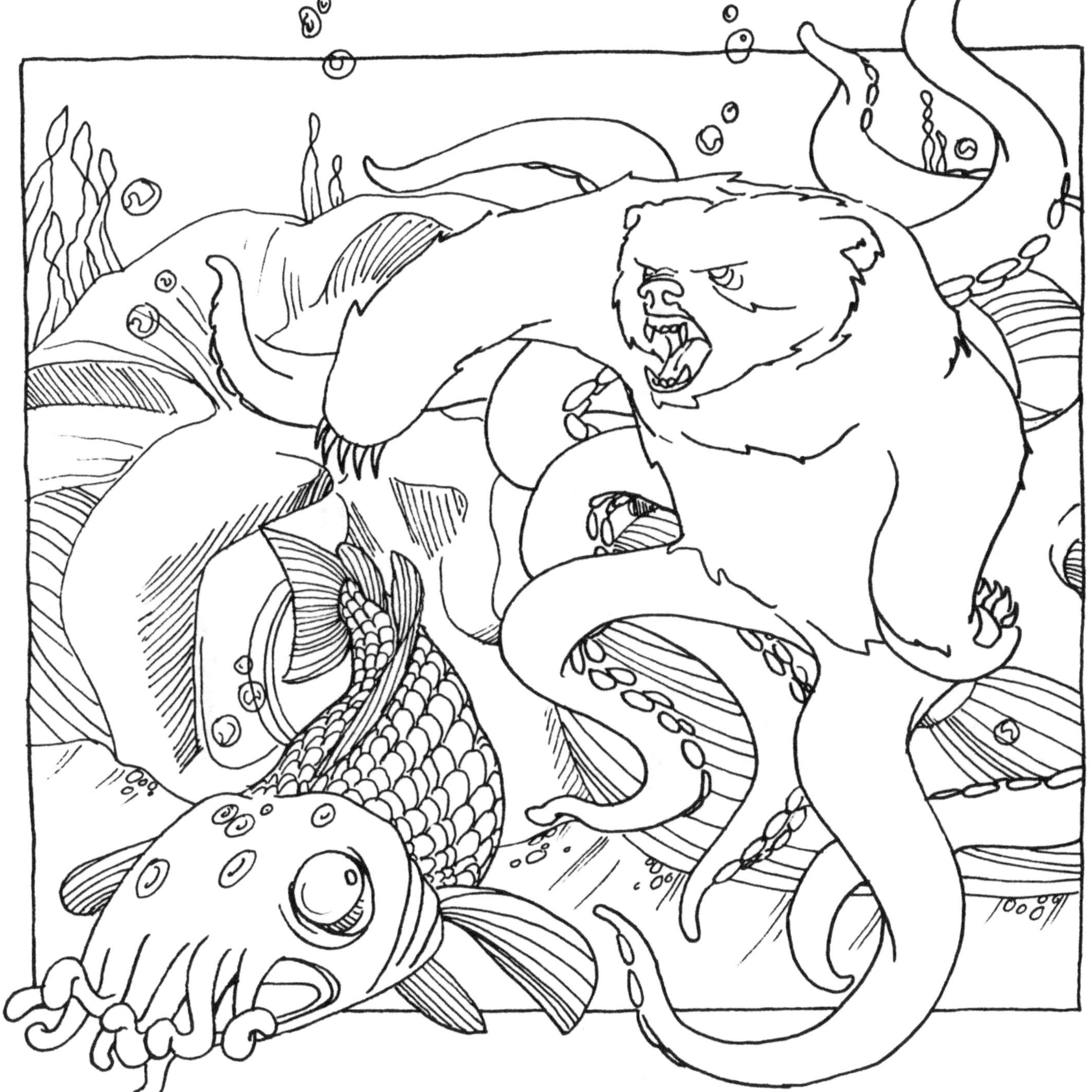

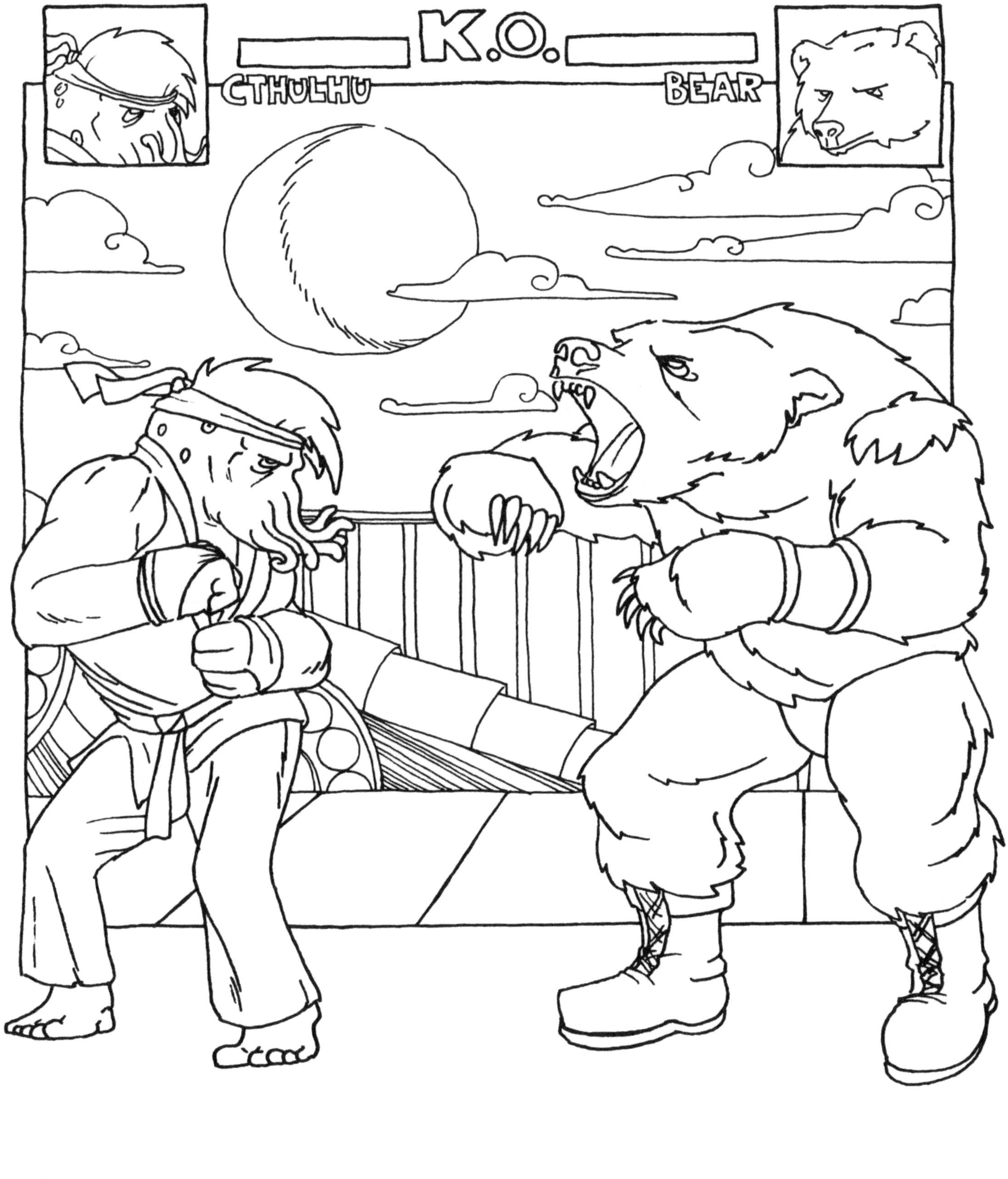
K.O.
CTHULHU
BEAR

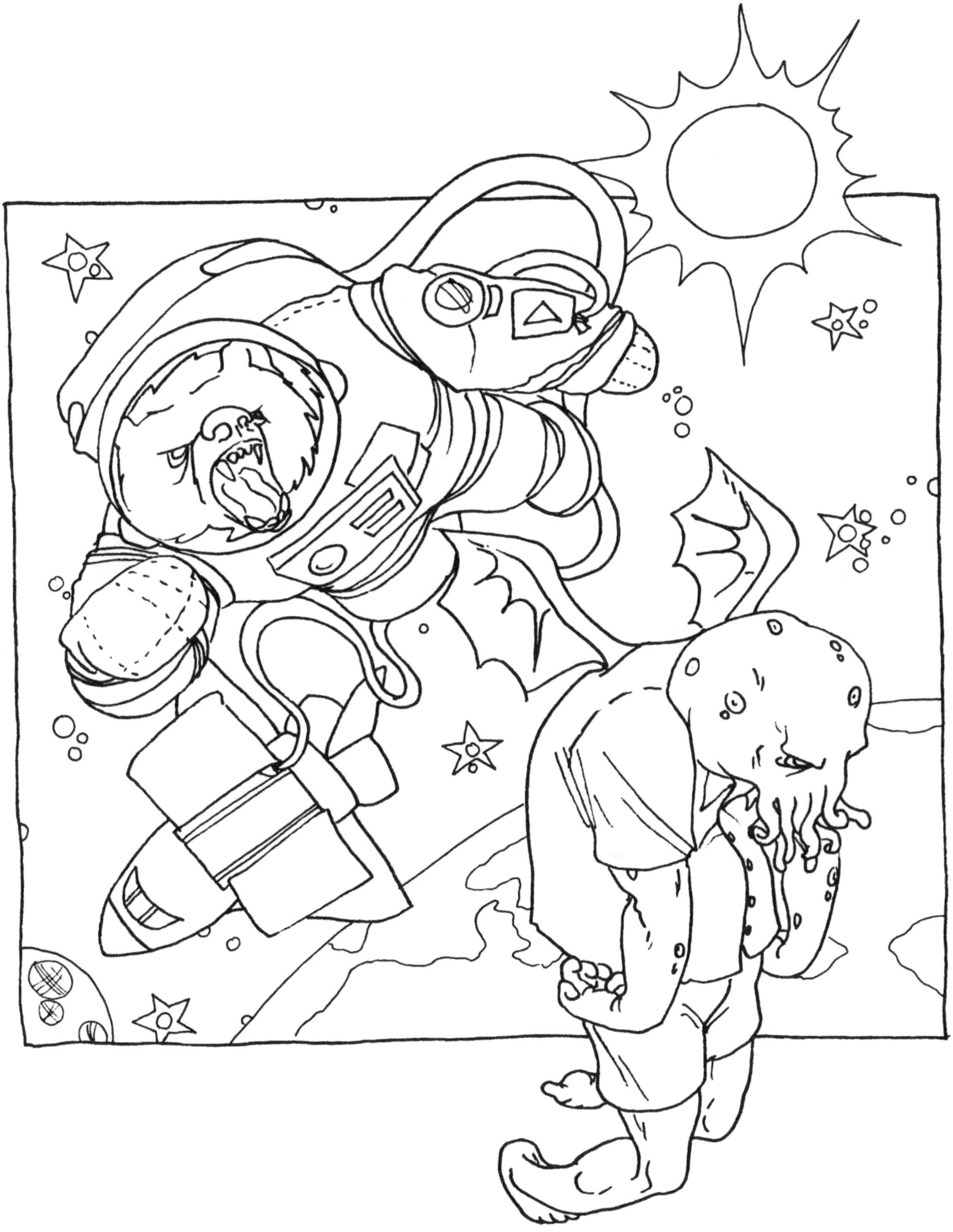

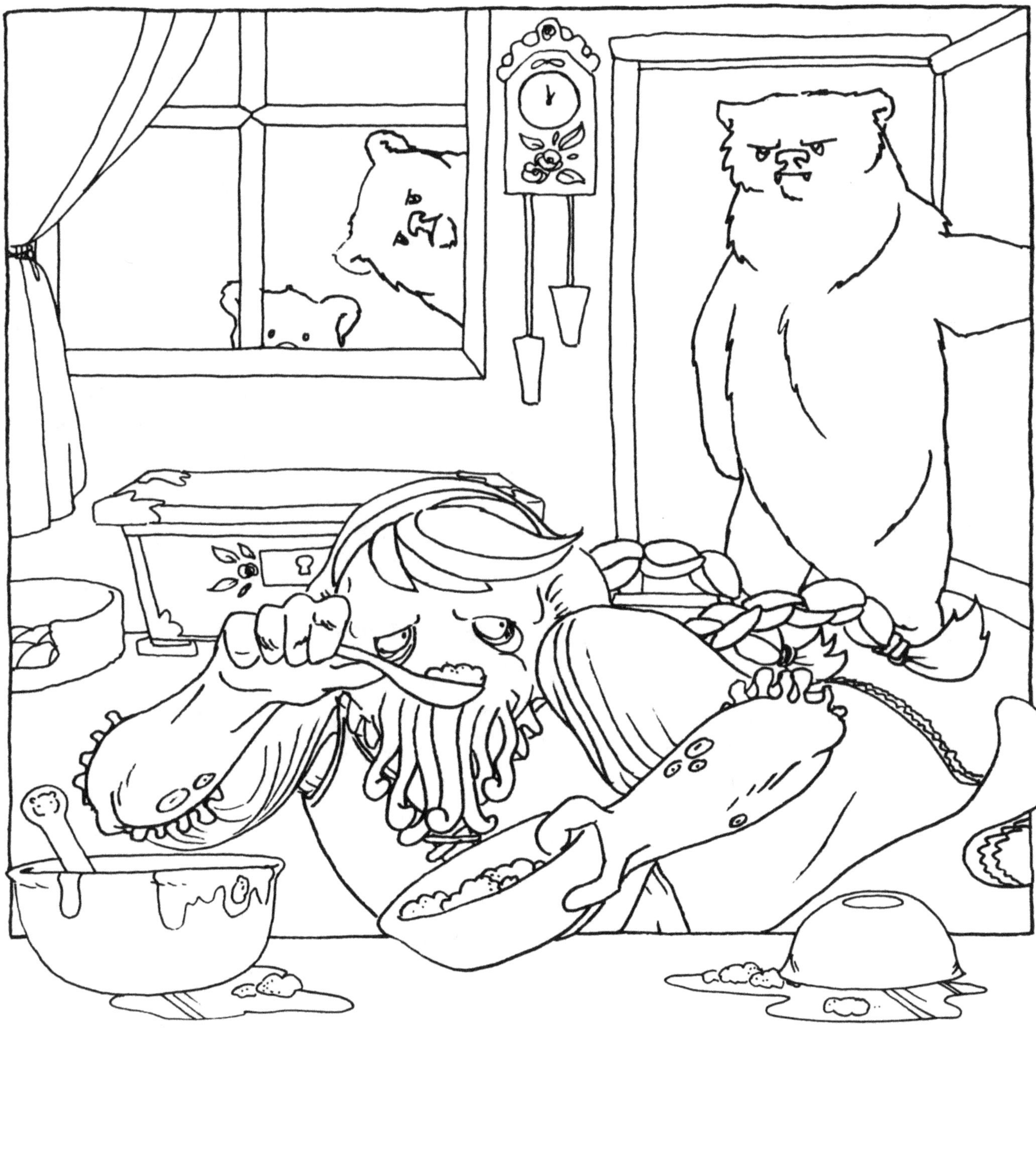

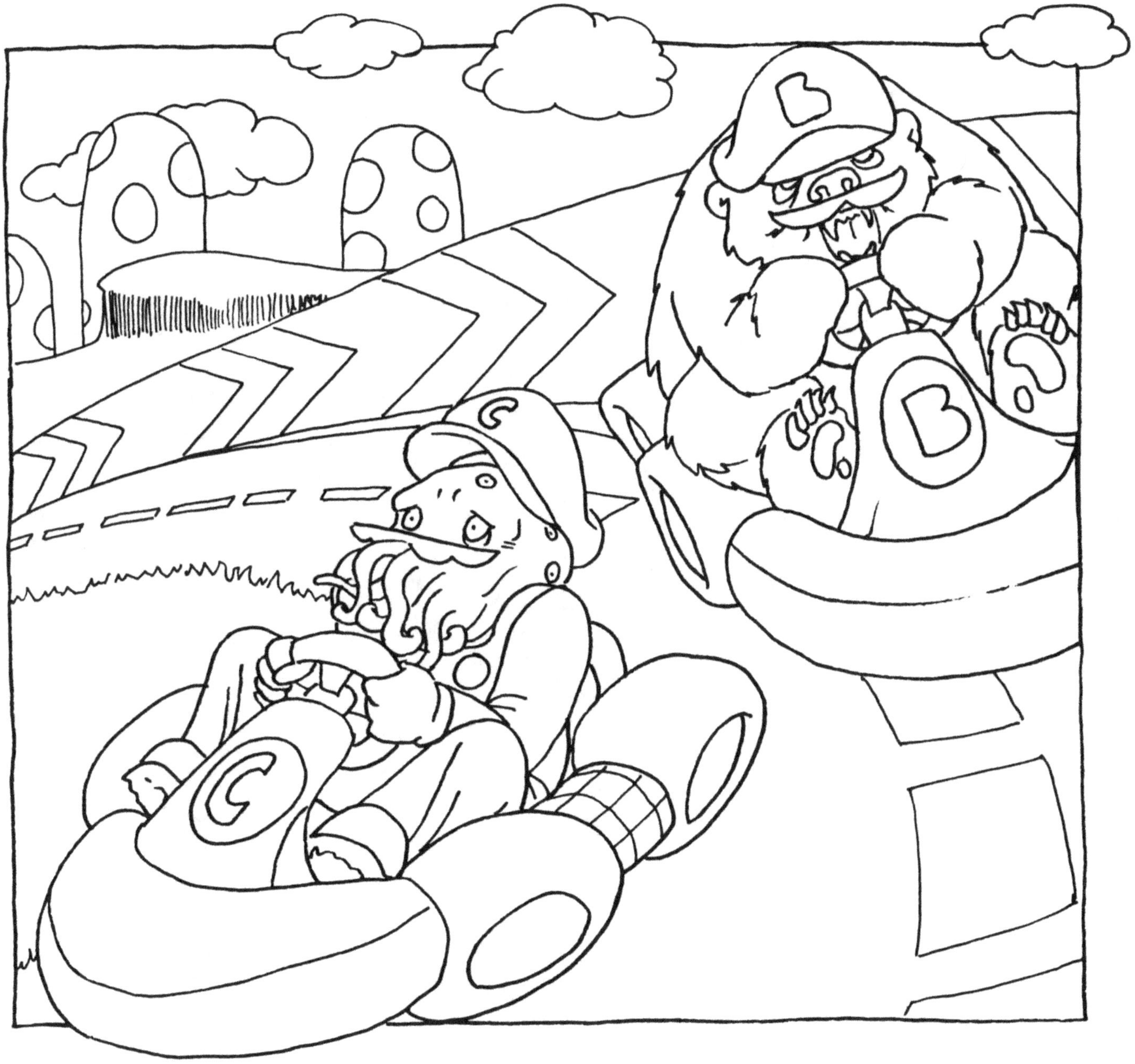
B
B
C
C

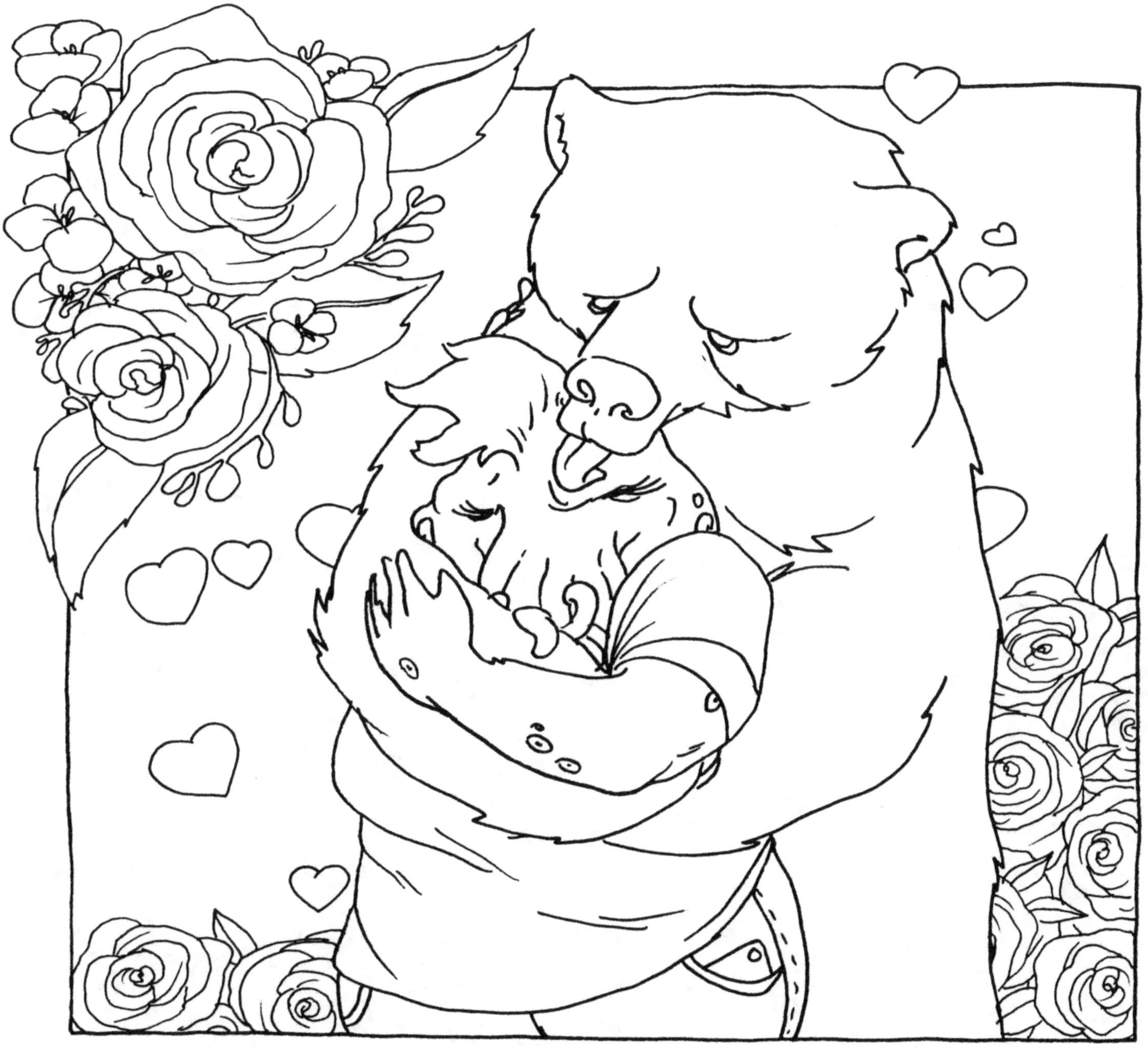

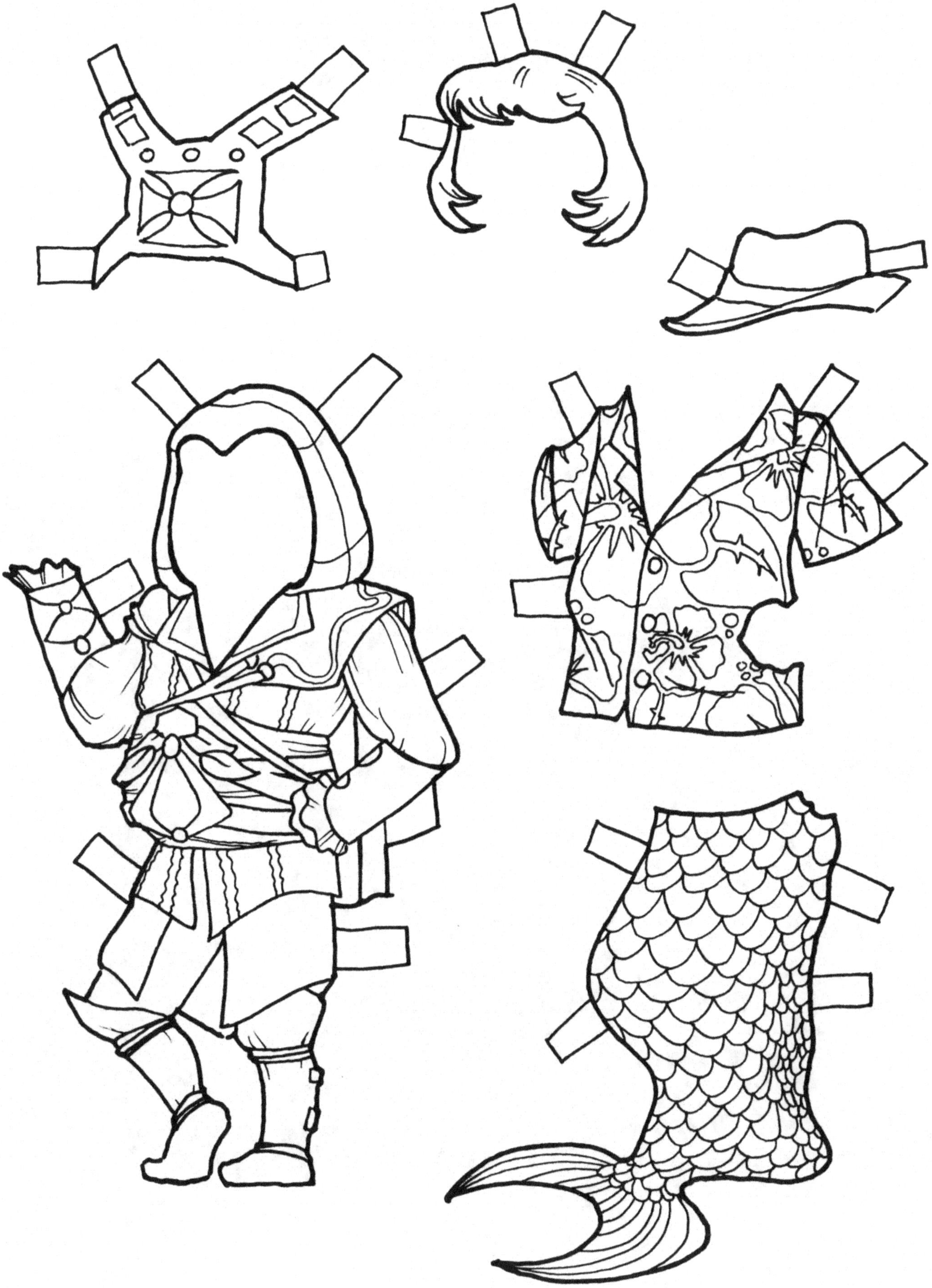

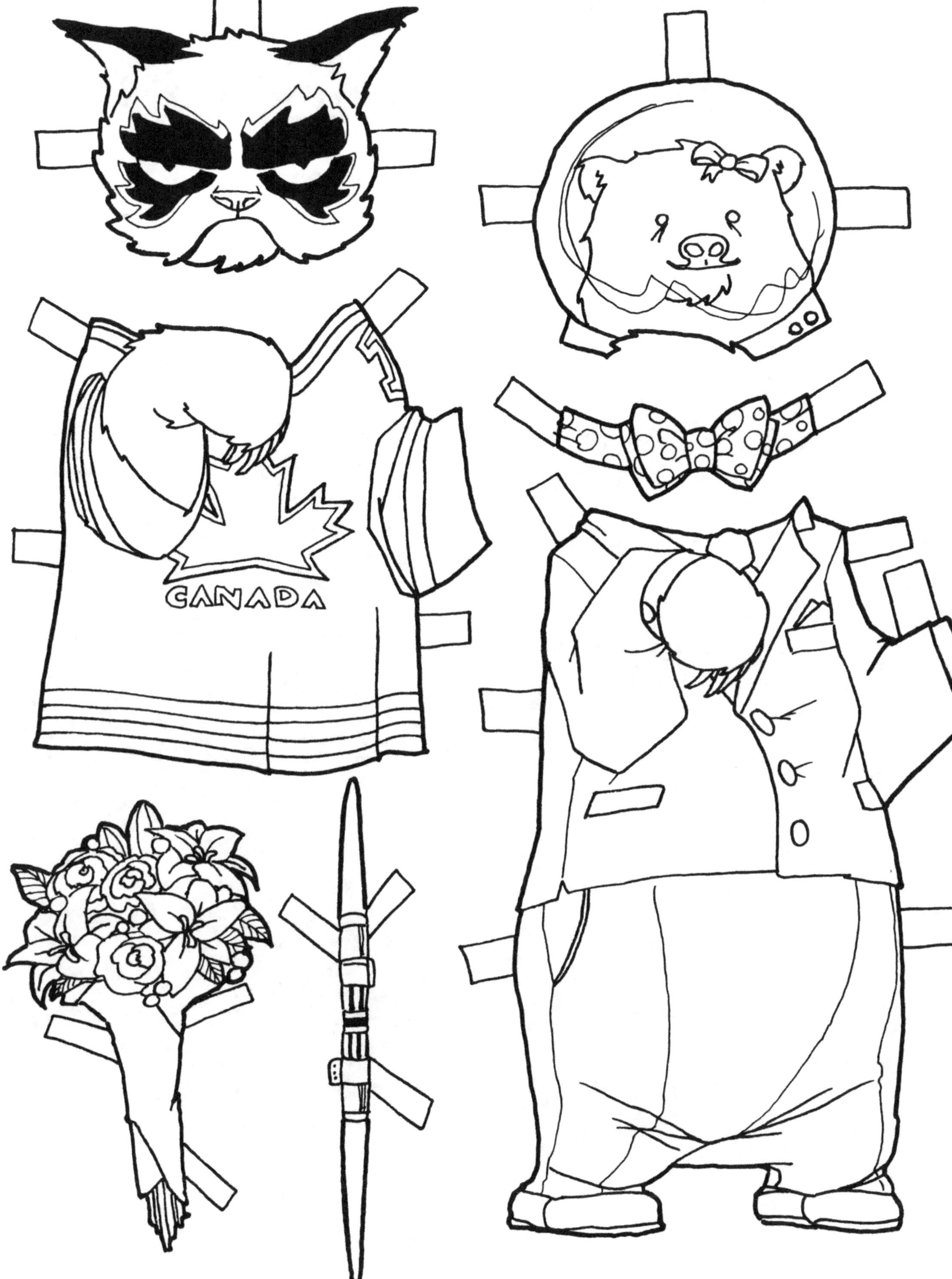
CANADA

www.ingramcontent.com/pod-product-compliance
Lightning Source LLC
Chambersburg PA
CBHW081609170526
45166CB00009B/2889
*9781500476656*